The Manager's Pocket Guide to Effective Writing

Steve Gladis, Ph.D.

HRD Press ❖ Amherst, Massachusetts

Production services by Jean Miller
Cover design by Eileen Klockars

ISBN 0-87425-479-5

Printed in Canada

Dedication

*To Don Gallehr
for being my mentor
and for teaching me about
writing.*

TABLE OF CONTENTS

INTRODUCTION

OVERVIEW

A Manager's Pocket Guide to Effective Writing is a how-to-write book. Intended for managers, the Guide works well as a self-directed learning text, but it can also be used as the basis for business in-service training. The book's primary purpose is to teach the writing process using a step-by-step method that takes the mystery out of writing.

The book divides the writing process into ten steps, from the development of the idea (exploring) to the final edit (ending). Each step builds on the previous one, and each chapter ends with a Writing Workshop. The Workshop consists of writing objectives and writing exercises, developing one specific memorandum report from chapter to chapter to illustrate the workshop steps of the writing process.

HOW TO USE THIS BOOK

This book is designed to be flexible. You can use it to review your own writing process, and you can recommend it to those who, by virtue of their own particular schedules, must work alone. You can also confidently use it as a training text.

The exercises at the end of the chapters are designed for hands-on instruction. They are direct and simple, but are very effective in teaching the writing process. When I teach workshops from this text, I assign the exercises for in-class work as well as homework.

I developed the Writing Illustration as a modeling device to show what each step in the writing process might look like. I have found that when people concretely visualize what an assignment is supposed to look like, their writing anxiety is reduced. The Writing Illustration is located at the very end of each chapter, following the writing exercise.

Those managers who must work on their own can use the text without the presence of an instructor. Because the steps are short and compartmentalized, participants can easily complete the assignments and send them to a trainer for review and quick comment.

I have used this text with excellent results in a one-week format for in-service training. I ask learners to come to the training with a particular piece of writing in mind. And, I ask that the writing be important to them— something they need to get done but (for one reason or another) haven't yet been able to complete. Thus, when they come to training, they have something they *need* and *want* to complete. Whether you're working alone or with a group, you can vastly improve your writing with this Pocket Guide.

Steve Gladis

PREFACE

I am a baby boomer whose earliest education took place in a Catholic grammar school. I learned the basics there: reading, writing, and arithmetic. But rather than tell you *what* I learned, I'd like to explain *how* I learned— particularly how I learned to write. See if it sounds familiar.

I had a teacher, Sister Mary Immaculate Conception. Like most teachers of her day, Sister demanded that her students learn all the rules of spelling, punctuation, and grammar that govern the English language. With that jumble of rules balanced precariously in my mind (much of it slipping and crashing on my cerebrum's floor), I was expected to write the perfect sentence—one that had all the words spelled right, all the grammar correct, and the penmanship perfect. I was rarely able to do all that, and when I did not, Sister let me know.

I'm not criticizing Sister; rather, I wish to point out that her theory of writing, popular in her day, was a one-step process. Such a process demands perfection and can produce at least among us not-so-perfect people, a sense of failure. A policy that demands perfection the first time can eventually produce writers who are afraid to put a pen to paper for fear of failure.

Let me confess: far from being perfect, I have a host of writing problems. The two that have plagued me since birth are spelling and penmanship. However, I have no respect for a person who can spell a word only one way—it shows a sad lack of imagination! And I've always had a problem with my penmanship. When I was young I didn't like the way my writing looked on paper, so I wrote as little as possible. Many people suffer from these and other problems that inhibit their writing. What's the answer to such problems in a day when we want to be accurate, yet creative?

Writing is a multi-stepped process, rather than a do-or-die, one-step proposition. Understanding this will remove much of the anxiety people experience when they write. Let me explain: If I have this idea that Sister is looking over my shoulder like a judge waiting to pass the final sentence, how can I write creatively? After all, I might be hanged at a moment's notice. On the other hand, if I know I'll have some time to work through the process step by step (and I know I can keep Sister, the judge, from looking over my shoulder until I've finished the product), I certainly have more of a chance at success. A writing process like this takes the pressure off exactness.

So, what *is* this writing process? Simply put, it's writing in steps. It's breaking down writing into a series of definable steps and tackling them one at a time. ***A Manager's Pocket Guide to Effective Writing*** will help reduce your writing anxiety and get you writing, because it divides writing into doable steps. I've broken down the process into ten manageable steps:

- selecting
- exploring
- fastwriting
- surveying
- hunting
- writing
- revising
- rewriting
- testing
- ending

Each step leads slowly and safely to the next. The end product will be every bit as perfect as the one Sister demanded. Yet the Guide allows you, the writer, to have some fun along the way, and still keep Sister from looking over your shoulder, at least for a while.

This book consists of ten chapters, each with a self-directed or group-centered assignment called "Writing Workshop," geared to take you from thinking about your idea to editing your final draft.

Chapter 1 looks at how you should prepare to write. Called **Selecting**, this chapter explores the early decisions you must make **before** you write, and what questions you'll need to ask yourself in order to give your writing a focus.

Chapter 2, **Exploring**, considers how your mind works, particularly how it works subconsciously. You'll examine the database you've collected in your own mind and determine how to access it. The chapter delves into the functions of collecting and connecting, and looks at how you as a manager/writer can use both to your advantage before ever putting pen to paper.

Chapter 3, **Fastwriting**, introduces you to four fastwriting techniques that let you put your ideas on paper quickly, thus helping to reduce your writing anxiety. This chapter describes the techniques of freewriting, freelisting (or brainstorming), webbing, and finally, freespeaking, the newest of these techniques.

Chapter 4, **Surveying**, teaches you how to scan your fast-written draft for ideas. Surveying finds out what you know and don't know about your topic; it finds the holes in your writing. You'll take care of filling these holes in Chapter 5.

Chapter 5, **Hunting**, introduces you to the techniques of gathering information from outside sources: people, and written material. You'll also learn how to develop the all-important focus statement.

Chapter 6, **Writing**, teaches you how to integrate your newly acquired information into your next draft.

Chapter 7, **Revising**, provides you with the first critical look at your writing. You'll examine your writing structure carefully and prepare it for reader comprehension. In this chapter you'll learn how to write clear paragraphs and how to link them together.

Chapter 8, **Rewriting**, helps you put your writing into a logical structure. You'll learn how to construct and integrate the introduction, the body, and the conclusion.

Chapter 9, **Testing**, shows you how to use others to improve your writing. This chapter examines the writing-broker concept and the COACH system. Each will help you improve your writing by using the help of others.

Chapter 10, **Ending**, provides handy clean-up editing tips, so you can high-polish your writing.

Each chapter ends with a Writing Work-shop consisting of teaching objectives, writing exercises, and a single Writing Illustration, that runs throughout the book to help you to stay on track, whether working with a group or alone. If you follow these easy steps, you will find yourself with a polished piece of writing in short order.

1.

SELECTING

SELECTING

Writing is thinking on a piece of paper. But you don't have to pen words or pound a keyboard to write. Much of the writing process can be done in your head. **Selecting**, the first and very important step in the writing process, often takes place in the mind. Of course, sometimes (especially at work) you cannot "select" your topic: The boss tells you to write a memo or you have a report that's due, or your own need dictates a specific topic (for example, you might need to ask for more staff). Any one of a hundred reasons can prevent you from selecting your own topic. But thousands of times you *can* and *do* select your topic. Selecting involves asking yourself some familiar questions about your topic: Who? Why? When and Where? What and How?

Good **selecting** means considering who you're writing for (the audience), why you're writing (the purpose), when and where you're writing (timing), what you're writing about (personal interest), and how you need to package it (format).

WHO?

First, *who* is your audience? Targeting and profiling your audience helps you select an appropriate topic and writing style. For example, when you write to your boss about a new office policy, you may be much more formal than when you write to your staff about that same policy. The way you write will likely be determined by the person(s) for whom it is intended. If you think a critical eye will read your writing, you will need to write with formal precision. Consider the police officer who writes a report that a defense attorney will scrutinize later: the audience will be more than critical, they will be adversarial, actively seeking flaws. Thus, police writing must remain cold and factual—it should leave nothing to interpretation.

Writing to any critical audience, even an adversarial one, is difficult, but you can easily accomplish it by using a process of dilution. Don't direct early drafts to the boss or the defense attorney; rather, direct them to a sympathetic associate or a friend. After you get some preliminary reactions, you can tighten and improve your draft through revising and editing. We'll talk in depth about how to do this in later chapters.

WHY?

Once you've decided *who*, ask yourself *why*? Why am I writing? What do I want the audience to do or think after they read my writing? Your purpose is the goal, the target of your writing. If you want your audience to have background on a topic (background for an annual shareholders' meeting, for example), then give facts. Facts are the building blocks of informational writing. If, however, you want to persuade the reader, you must support those facts with reasons and evidence—the mortar that cements facts into a persuasive structure. If you want your boss to buy a new piece of equipment, you'll need to show why the purchase should be made. Giving facts such as the equipment's specs and stats might be good for background, but they are not enough to persuade. Along with this supporting data, you must provide reasons that will logically persuade and so enhance your chances of getting what you want.

Before you begin writing, try the following technique. At the top of your paper write the word **purpose**. Now write, in one sentence, what you believe your purpose to be. For example: "The purpose of this memo is to provide management with in-depth background data on super widgets." Or "The purpose of this report is to provide data and analysis to support the recommendation to buy a new widget press for the production plant." Each of these purpose statements focuses the writer and reader on the end product **right from the start**. Each provides a fixed frame of reference.

To illustrate how such a purpose line can work for the reader as well as the writer, consider the purpose of the following paragraph:

> *The procedure is actually quite simple. First, you arrange things into different groups. Of course, one pile may be sufficient depending on how much there is to do. If you have to go somewhere else due to lack of facilities, that is the next step; otherwise you are pretty well set. It is important not to overdo things. That is, it is better to do too few things at once than too many. In the short run this may not seem important, but complications can easily arise. A mistake can be expensive as well. At first the whole procedure will seem complicated. Soon, however, it will become just another facet of life. It is difficult to foresee any end to the necessity for this task in the immediate future, but*

then, one can never tell. After the procedure is completed, one arranges the materials into different groups again. Then they can be put into their appropriate places. Eventually they will be used once more, and the whole cycle will then have to be repeated. However, that is part of life.*

OK, what's it about? About as clear as mud, you say? Now, reread the passage after reading the following purpose statement: *"The purpose of this memo is to outline the proper procedure to do laundry."* Make more sense now? Why? Because you, the reader, knew the purpose up front.

---

*John D. Bransford and Marcia K. Johnson, "Consideration of Some Problems of Comprehension," in *Visual Information Processing,* ed. William G. Chase (New York: Academic Press, 1973), p. 400.

WHEN AND WHERE?

Now, with the who (the audience) and the why (the purpose) firmly in mind, you need to think about the **when** and the **where**—the timing of the topic. Sometimes a topic will float, while other times it will sink. Political considerations always influence a piece of writing. What happened before your boss read the proposal? Did she see a big article in the morning newspaper that talked about how poorly widgets perform? If she did, you're going to need a most persuasive document to overcome this poor timing. Depending on your topic's importance, you may have to wait a few days, weeks, or even months before sur-facing it. Not everything has to be written or submitted right now. Timing can be crucial to the success of any project.

To consider timing, ask yourself these questions: What does the reader think of this topic? Has anything recently happened that pertains to the topic? Is now the best time (Monday, Friday, vacation time, etc.) to bring up this topic?

The boss's schedule, need, or both can affect whether or not your memo gets her consideration. If the boss seems rushed, harried, or distracted, wait for a more relaxed time to hand over an important proposal. This will help reduce the risk of an out-and-out **no**. As a reverse strategy, you might try running simple things through during hectic times to get a quick **yes** or **no**. Just consider the risks whenever you think about timing.

WHAT?

In the Selecting step, consider **what** you write. Remember to select a topic that interests you. When writers "own" (have vital interest in) their writing, they create a much better product. Compare a rented home to one that is owned: The difference is obvious. **Ownership evokes pride.** If you have a personal investment in something, generally you'll work harder to do a better job. So it is with writing.

Now, we all have to write about things that aren't at the top of our "ownership list." It's hard to feel a deep sense of ownership when you write a memo about vacation leave times for the department, unless, of course, you need to convince the boss to let you go. But other memos may mean a lot to you: new ideas for capital expansion, thoughts on new markets to explore, analyses of profitability. Further, if you, as a manager, instill a sense of ownership in your subordinates, the quality of their writing will rise dramatically.

HOW?

Finally, one often-overlooked element of writing is the actual physical document. *How* something looks can be as important as who, why, when, where, and what you write.

The reader has certain structural expectations that you must meet. If you submit your writing in an unfamiliar or incorrect format, the reader may reject it immediately or stop reading before finishing the document.

To help you visualize how something should look, examine samples of previous memos and reports on the same topic. Don't copy the style if the language is mediocre, but do copy the format. It makes sense to meet the reader's expectations; to do so is part of being a good writer.

Writing Workshop #1
Selecting

Writing is a skill; you can't learn to write by reading about it. You've got to write to become better.

You seldom have the luxury of writing about what you want at work. However, you'll get that chance in this workshop.

You've probably felt the urge to make a meaningful suggestion or express a long-held opinion about something. You may have wanted to inform, persuade, or inspire the boss, a peer, or a subordinate.

Choose a job-related topic you'd like to write about—something you can work with throughout this book—to refine and revise. If you're already in the middle of a writing project, you can work on that.

Objectives

1. To establish what the writer wants or needs to write about.

2. To articulate the reaction that the writer wants the reader to have to the writing.

3. To list audience personality traits and needs before the writing begins.

Activities

STEP 1

Let your thoughts run wild. Pretend you're writing (freewriting) an informal note to a friend. Begin writing for ten minutes, using the following statement as a prompt: "I would like most to write to_____ (person) about . . ." Don't be afraid to take on your dream. It may be to tell the boss you've got a better way to build a mousetrap. For a start, write to more than one audience (boss, peers, and subordinates) about more than one idea. You're simply digging for a topic aimed at a potential audience. Take time and have fun.

STEP 2

Underline or bracket the ideas that most appeal to you. Now, number them in the order of their priority, with "one" as the highest priority. Choose the idea that most appeals to you and that may also have some impact on the company. Also consider the timing of your topic. Will it appeal to your reader at this time? Be sure the topic lends itself to substantial development.

STEP 3

To determine your purpose in writing, ask yourself what you want the reader to know or do after reading your report. Try completing the following sentence:

"After reading my report, the reader should know or do the following . . . "

STEP 4

Who will read this report? What is their educational background, economic status, relationship to you, interest in the topic, needs (power, control, etc.), immediate goals, personal problems?

Writing as quickly as you can for ten minutes, try to develop an accurate profile of your reader. If it will help, use the following prompt:

"My reader is_____(my peer, my boss, etc.), and this is what I know about him/her . . ."

STEP 5

Find a partner or two for the writing process. Your partners can be friends, colleagues, or family members—people you trust and whose opinions you value. You will use them to test your writing—to bounce ideas off of. Discuss your audience needs with your writing process partners. Revise your descriptions to take their feedback into account.

Writing Illustration

NOTE: To illustrate each step in the writing process, a single example will be developed and refined throughout the book. From idea conception to final editing, you'll see principles demonstrated concretely and realistically.

STEP 1: DIGGING FOR A TOPIC

"I would most like to write to my boss about improving my department: I need space; I need computers; I need training; I need travel and funding.

"I would like to write to my peers about the help I need from them on training executive groups or developing joint research projects or designing a new integrated curriculum.

"I would like to write to subordinates to tell them they should be innovative and seek advanced training, or to ask them about their hopes and aspirations for the future and about their career development."

STEP 2: NARROWING THE FIELD

"At this point I would underline and/or highlight the subject of computers, and also the idea about an integrated curriculum. I would probably end up choosing the one dealing with computers."

STEP 3: SEEKING A RESPONSE

"After reading the report, the reader, my boss, should (1) know what the needs are for computer training, and (2) approve a needs

assessment, which will be developed by an
outside consultant."

STEP 4: PROFILING THE AUDIENCE

"My reader is my boss and this is what I
know about her. She is a 42-year-old woman
who is very vocal and does not like to read
lengthy or complex proposals. Rather, she is
the kind of person who likes things short and
to the point. I guess, then, some sort of synopsis with the recommendations up front in my
proposal will help, because she doesn't want to
spend a lot of time wading through rhetoric.
But she does want the analysis done, so it
must be in there. Maybe some charts and/or
graphics would help pull it together for her.

"She is very experienced and is an excep-
tional instructor; she has been in teaching her
whole life; she likes new and innovative things
as opposed to stock and staid things. She also
likes to be in the forefront; *new* is a key word
for her; *innovative* is a key word for her. Words
like that would be trigger words, so I might
want to include those in my document. She
has a strong work ethic, and she is careful
about effort, time, and cost. She is loyal to the
organization and is basically a very ethical

person. She works hard and recognizes that effort in others. She used to be computer-phobic, but now she has started using hers more and more. She seems to be more involved in the process and more accepting to its indexing and database aspects, so I might want to use them as the basis for my proposal."

STEP 5

"Talked to Joe Schmo, a colleague of mine, and he said my boss was impressed with a recent board presentation by an outside consultant on integrated computer systems."

2.

EXPLORING

EXPLORING

You've answered the important selecting
questions and begun to write, even though
your paper remains sketchy. Now what do you
do? You need to explore what you've selected.
Like selecting, Exploring is a pre-writing exercise, designed primarily to make you think.
Remember, writing is thinking on paper. Therefore, including a step in your writing process
that allows for thinking is critical to good writing. This chapter examines how you collect and
store information, as well as how to connect it.

COLLECTING

First, consider how much information
you've collected over the years. If you are 25
years old, you've collected information for at
least 25 years. You have read, talked, touched,
tasted, smelled, heard, and seen a lot, piling up
experiences and storing this information deep
within your brain. All these bits of information
may not readily surface in your conscious
brain, but they do float somewhere in that
great reservoir: your subconscious.

For the sake of illustration, think of your
brain as an iceberg, with only its tip jutting
above the surface of the water. Below the

surface lies a massive, unseen base. The portion above the waterline represents our
conscious brain. Your subconscious is like the
massive base below the water level—out of
sight, but ever present. It is this subconscious
that stores so many collected ideas, some
more deeply than others. The ideas come
flooding in daily, especially in this age of information. TV, radio, faxes, newspapers, the
Internet, and computers themselves simply
increase the flood. You are at least vaguely
familiar with an enormous range of topics,
because in today's society you cannot avoid
being bombarded with information.

For example, let's say you want to hire a
new assistant for your office to help increase
its efficiency. Should you run down the street
to the library, or should you call in an efficiency
expert? Again, remember the iceberg analogy.
You've been part of the office for years,
collecting enormous amounts of information.
Why not begin with what you know, because
you probably know as much as anyone else
about this topic. In fact, you'll find that when
you do hire consultants in such a situation,
you'll learn that they spend a lot of time asking
you what *you* know. When they've finished
their evaluation, the results should not shock

you. Usually, they will simply **write down what you know**. So, in the exploring step, you should just act like a consultant and think about **what you know**. Probe your subconscious and put your findings on a piece of paper.

CONNECTING

How do you get started? First, you must understand the process called **connecting**. You've been collecting information for years. Connecting simply allows you to pull together all the pieces of this information. If you can only vaguely remember collecting information on a topic, you must give yourself time to let the stimulus of the project or topic rattle around in your subconscious. This time allows you to connect bits of information collected three years ago with bits collected three days ago. Time allows your brain to assemble a readout, much like that produced by a random search of a computer database. You input the topic, with the necessary parameters, and wait as your brain whirs, blinks, and connects. But you need to allow this processing time.

How much time? The answer depends on each situation, because sometimes you don't have time. The boss calls and tells you to write something, and you must react immediately. When you have only a couple of hours or a day to get a memo out, set aside part of that time for some subconscious thinking. Write the idea on a card and place it on your desk. Go out for a walk; talk with a friend; go out for lunch—all the time you'll be thinking and mentally writing. You'll be exploring.

But what about those many instances when you do have time? When you've got the chance, try "sleeping on it" (the idea). This will help enormously. Again, help yourself by writing the topic down on a three-by-five card and propping it on your desk. Casual glances during the day will continue to stimulate subconscious as well as conscious thoughts on the topic. Each time your mind receives this visual stimulus, it will perform a kind of minisearch and re-search.

But remember, because you must now give yourself "exploring" time, you may begin to procrastinate. Be careful: It's counterproductive to put off writing. Two weeks of stacking and reshuffling notes is procrastination, which does you no good. Your brain usually needs only a day for connecting.

With time to probe the subconscious, you'll experience a kind of thermodynamic phenomenon. Ideas will suddenly rise from the depths of the subconscious to the surface of the conscious. First, they simmer; then they bubble; and before long, they boil. You will know when you've reached this rolling-boil stage. You'll begin to mumble, even talk to yourself; your conscious mind will become intrigued by the idea, and you'll find yourself constantly drifting back to it. This phenomenon is a sure sign that you're getting ready to write.

Next, you may even begin to feel anxious, uneasy. Your mind is seeking to organize its random thoughts and is calling on you to nail them down in concrete terms — with words. Once you put your ideas on paper, you'll be able to order and clarify them.

Many people have written about writing apprehension or "writer's block." But you should understand that a certain amount of anxiety about writing is a normal and useful stimulus to writing. That is not to say that some writers don't get blocked. They do. However, most blocks come from not knowing how to get from the Exploring–prewriting stage to the Writing stage. The next chapter shows you how to overcome writer's block by using fastwriting techniques to get ideas on paper quickly.

Writing Workshop #2
Exploring

Not all writing takes place with a pen and a piece of paper, or at a computer. Some of the writing process takes place in your head while you are sitting, walking, running, or driving. Allow time for your ideas to bubble to the surface.

Objectives

1. To show how time helps mature an idea.

2. To demonstrate the process of mentally exploring a topic.

Activities

STEP 1
Take the topic you developed in Chapter 1 and write it out in big letters on several index cards. Put one on your desk and another in your car, or wherever you plan to spend time in the next day or two.

STEP 2

Now, go about your daily business, occasionally glancing at the cards.

STEP 3

If you want to write an idea or two on the card, OK. Just don't write too much yet. When you get jittery, even antsy, you're getting ready to write—and you will write in the next chapter, so hold on.

Writing Illustration

STEP 1: FOCUSING ON THE SUBJECT

> **Computers in Training**

STEP 2: THINKING ABOUT THE TOPIC

THINK!

STEP 3: JOTTING DOWN IDEAS

Computers in Training
Lesson Plans
Objectives
Database
Scheduling

3.

FASTWRITING

FASTWRITING

All writers face a critical point in the writing process after they have mentally explored a topic: physically beginning to write. Writers will sometimes do just about anything to avoid writing, from cleaning out briefcases and desktop drawers to sharpening pencils and rereading an article. And even when they do get started, you can hear the untimely crumple of paper and the snap of pencils as writer's block strikes—the unmistakable ogre of hesitation and anxiety rears itself precisely at this point during the writing process.

But never fear. There are several ways around the blocks in your path to writing. Here's the story of how one doctoral student solved his problems with writer's block. He had to finish his dissertation by a particular date or be forever a member of the ABD ("all but dissertation") Club, a club populated by doctoral students who complete all the course work for the degree but do not get over their writer's block in time to finish the final project.

This particular student was at a standstill, and it was a major stall. He went to a psychologist who, after hearing the student's

story, asked how much money the student had
in the bank. "$3,500," the student replied.

"Fine," replied the savvy psychologist.
"Make me out a check for the entire amount. I
will not cash it until one day after your dissertation is due, and only if you do not meet the
deadline. If you do finish on time, you get the
check back—except, of course, for my fee."

Bewildered by a sense of desperation, the
student gave the check to the psychologist.
Several months later, he successfully
completed his dissertation and retrieved his
check. Less, of course, a hefty fee.

This is one solution to writer's block, but
the risk is probably more than most are willing
to take on. As good alternatives, I suggest four
fastwriting techniques developed from practice
and research that will be just as effective as
the psychologist's method.

FREEWRITING

One of the most widely used techniques to
get ideas on paper quickly and effortlessly is
called *freewriting*. Like its name suggests,
freewriting relies on a relaxed, "free" mind,

much like the state of mind you may have when writing a letter to a trusted friend.

When you freewrite, don't worry about the mechanics of writing—just the ideas. This way, you won't get bogged down in the details of grammar, punctuation, and spelling while producing an initial draft. The technique is quite simple: just put pen to paper and write as if you are telling a story.

It's important to pretend that you're writing to a good friend because research has found that an over-developed sense of audience (an intimidating audience, such as the supervisor or chairman of the board) can bring on writer's block and stop the writing process before it ever begins. Just remember the last time you had to write a letter to or (even worse) *for* the boss. If you're like so many others, you found yourself scratching out words, stopping and starting and generally spending an enormous amount of time writing. By mentally assuming that the initial audience is just a good friend, you remove the judge-like authority figure in your mind. And guess what the results are? Fastwriting. It's sure a lot easier to write a memo to your old friend Jack or Jean than to the chairman of the board, so why not freewrite the first draft to a friend?

The rules for freewriting are simple:

1. Choose your favorite pen, paper, chair, and place to write—they all make a difference.

2. Imagine a good friend, one who knows that you can't spell all the words in the dictionary and don't know all the grammar rules in the world—someone who won't judge you.

3. Start writing to your friend (Dear Jean), and don't stop for anything until you have explained your ideas in everyday language.

4. Don't correct spelling, punctuation, or grammar. Just let the ideas roll out of the pen.

Freewriting is like priming a pump: it gets the ideas flowing. And with those ideas comes language. It will be easier to think and express your thoughts if your audience is nonthreatening. Freewriting unleashes the power of your brain by removing the anxiety that locked it there in the first place. To practice freewriting, simply sit down and write two or three letters to friends you haven't corresponded with in a while. Indeed, letter writing is the purest form of freewriting.

FREELISTING

Some people don't like to write letters, and some people don't like freewriting. Don't worry if you're in that group. Try freelisting—a kind of brainstorming. Let's say you have to write a report, and you just don't know where to begin. Sound familiar? Simply list the main topic at the top of a blank sheet of paper. Spray the page with related ideas; don't worry about their order and, whatever you do, don't laugh at your own ideas. Some of the wildest ones may end up being the best! Then step back, look at each idea, and copy it on a separate piece of paper or file card. Use that single idea as the basis for some heavy-duty brainstorming. You'll begin to break down the component ideas and, in a very informal and free way, you'll be forming the basis of a working outline.

Let's use the topic of public affairs as an example. Let's freelist about public affairs:

- Press relations
- Publications
- Speeches
- Correspondence
- Research

Now let's take one component idea—press relations—and break it down:

- Press conferences
- Liaison
- Press releases
- News inquiries

Continue the process for each component idea until you cannot break each one down any further. Let's look at some of the steps for freelisting:

1. Sit down at a favorite place with a favorite pen. Get comfortable.

2. Write the main topic on the top of the page and free-associate any ideas that come into your head; write them down as quickly as you can.

3. Step back from your original list and try to check off the main ideas. You'll find that some insignificant ones have been listed with the main ideas. Don't worry; the concept is not to filter anything out initially, but simply to get the ideas flowing.

4. List each main idea on a separate sheet of paper or index card and repeat the brainstorming and freelisting for each of these subtopics.

5. Repeat the process until you can no longer break down your subtopics.

Freelisting provides you with the basic ideas, and perhaps even the foundation for an initial outline. It can be done quickly, alone, and anywhere—on a matchbook cover, a cocktail napkin, or on a scrap piece of newspaper.

WEBBING

This third fastwriting technique will appeal to those who are visual. Just as its name suggests, Webbing is a way of weaving your ideas together the way a spider spins a web. Spin *your* web by writing the main topic in the middle of a paper and circling the word. Next, draw lines to bubbles of ideas that relate to the main ideas. Pretty soon you will have a weblike sketch on your paper. You'll easily *see* where you need more research and where your ideas are highly developed. More importantly, you'll be able to *see* your report—to visualize your writing.

Let's try an example to see how it works. We'll explore the topic of corporate fitness programs:

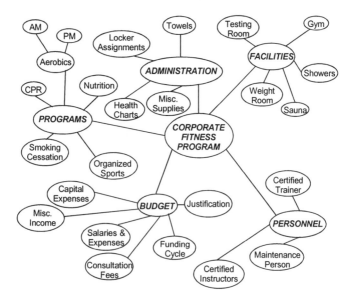

Quickly, you can see a piece of writing taking shape. This piece, in fact, might whip the entire company into shape.

Let's review the Webbing steps:

1. Don't think about any particular audience.

2. Write your main topic in the middle of the page.

3. Draw lines off the central topic to related ideas.

4. Continue to break down sub-ideas by drawing off lines to related sub-ideas until you can spin your web no further.

5. Step back from your web and reinspect it with a fresh eye.

FREESPEAKING

The last fastwriting technique will appeal to people with a good ear. If you've ever said, "I'm just thinking out loud," or "I'm just talking to hear myself think," then you've already experienced freespeaking.

Freespeaking is similar to dictation, but it flows more freely. To freespeak, you need to use a tape recorder and pretend you're talking to someone—a specific audience, a trusted friend. This technique allows you to discuss your ideas with an audience and to develop and analyze them as you speak. The initial words may come out awkwardly, but after a sentence or two, the speaker who is comfortable with speaking skills will, in no time, roll out ideas and create a "draft." For obvious reasons, this technique seems to appeal to people who like to talk. Again, keep your tone conversational; you do not need to impress anyone.

You should freespeak until you finish your piece. Usually it takes no more than ten minutes to produce a ten-page, typewritten document. When you finish freespeaking, transcribe what you've "written." I suggest transcribing the recording *exactly,* so you can get the richness of your spoken language into your written language. Then be prepared to make major revisions to make your message clear to others. This technique takes advantage of the strongly practiced speaking skills we all generally possess; it uses them to produce the foundation of the written piece. The disadvantage of this technique is that spoken drafts often contain a great deal of repetition. Thus, they require a lot of editing.

Here's a brief review of Freespeaking:

1. Set up a tape recorder in a quiet room.

2. Assume that your audience is a trusted friend.

3. Speak freely, in a conversational way.

4. Transcribe your tape recording.

PREFERENCES

Remember the old saying, "Different horses for different courses"? Well, that saying applies to fastwriting techniques. What works well for one person may not work well for another. Some people are holistic and prefer Freewriting. Others are analytical and prefer Freelisting. Some are visual and prefer Webbing. And others are aural and prefer Freespeaking.

Each of these fastwriting techniques will appeal to different people. While no single technique necessarily outshines the others, each offers a place to start writing. They free the mind's ideas and get them on paper—a critical event because creating the "raw material" often causes writers great anxiety. By using these ideas, as others have, the power of writing quickly and with enjoyment will be yours.

Writing Workshop #3
Fastwriting

A blank page can intimidate even the most experienced writer. But several techniques can help you break through writer's block and get your words flowing on paper. Once you've tried each of these, you may find one that you prefer. At first, however, try them all.

Objectives

1. To develop a discovery draft to find out what you know about your topic.

2. To help relieve writing anxiety.

3. To discover the creative force of writing.

Activities

STEP 1: FREEWRITING

Choose any topic on your list, other than the one you've selected for your report, and freewrite about it as though you were writing a letter to a friend. Freewrite for about 10 minutes. Remember, don't stop and don't worry about punctuation, spelling, or grammar. Just write.

STEP 2: BRAINSTORMING/FREELISTING

Select another topic. Now, break it down into some main headings. Break down those headings further, then break those subheads further into sub-subheads, etc., until you can't break them down any more. Work on this exercise for ten minutes. Does an outline begin to emerge for you?

STEP 3: WEBBING

Select another topic. This time use the webbing technique to form a map. Write your topic in the middle of a page and draw connecting boxes or bubbles of subtopics to it. Again, as you did while brainstorming, keep breaking down headings to form a "picture" of your writing project. Take ten minutes to do this exercise.

STEP 4: FREESPEAKING

Select a fourth and final topic. Now, simply give a partner some paper and a pen and begin to talk freely about your topic. Your partner should listen and take notes. Keep talking for five minutes. This exercise works even better with a tape recorder. If you have one available, use it; then, simply transcribe your freespeaking to serve as a discovery draft.

STEP 5: EVALUATION AND DISCOVERY DRAFT

Now that you've had the chance to try each technique with a different topic, you may find that you prefer one method of fastwriting over the others. Decide which technique you like the most and use it on the topic you've selected for your report. This fastwriting draft will serve as a discovery draft and the starting point for your paper.

Writing Illustration

NOTE: To demonstrate clearly each different fastwriting technique, I will use only one topic, **Computers in Training**. Notice how each method generates a set of ideas.

STEP 1: FREEWRITING

Dear Joe,

I'm writing you this letter because I need a friendly ear to listen to my idea. I feel pretty stupid because I know I won't actually be mailing this thing to you. So, here goes. As you know, I'm the training coordinator for our company, and a large part of my job centers on teaching executives to speak and write. Now, mind you, they're all pretty articulate, but my job is to help them polish any rough edges—through a training program.

My work would be tremendously enhanced if I were able to purchase some computers and much needed software. To refresh your memory, I've got six instructors who report to me. I require each of them to have a lesson plan on file for each of their blocks of instruction. The tough part, Joe, is that we've only got one staff assistant for all of us users. It's impossible for him to keep up. Thus, we have a lot of classes for which we have no lesson plans on file, no way to easily track everyone's schedule, and no access to computer-based training software to enhance instruction. I thought if we could get more computers and the right software, it would help take the pressure off the staff assistant and give the instructors a good assist . . .

STEP 2: FREELISTING

Company Training with Computers

STEP 3: WEBBING

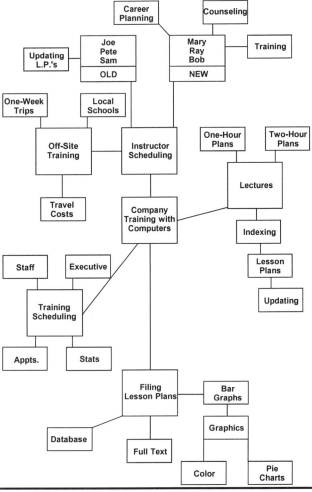

STEP 4: FREESPEAKING

"Hi, Joe. I am a training coordinator for a large multinational ping-pong ball manufacturing company. Our training center is located in a suburb. I teach communication skills here to executives who need to make presentations in the field. I think we could do a better job for these executives if we had computers in our facility. We could use them in a couple of ways. I could use a database system to index a lot of the lesson plans and to index the various groups that we teach, then just retrieve the information for quarterly reports, etc. This would really help my operation because it would get rid of file storage problems, eliminate a lot of unnecessary paper, and let all of us instantly retrieve anything we wanted. It would really help the efficiency of the office. I can also use the computer for scheduling. My office needs a lot of scheduling to keep it running efficiently. Right now it's being done by hand—it's inefficient—and there are software packages out that could solve the whole problem. I could get a report on the status of anything I wanted, like program progress in the office. I know my instructors could also benefit from some computer-based training programs that are on the market and are transforming the industry. The right CBT package could help free up my instructors' time while enhancing the trainees' experiences. I don't know much about this kind of equipment—the type of technical equipment out there or even how much it costs—but I do know there are ABC computers and XYZ computers available that might be good. I'll have to find out more about the equipment and its capabilities before I can actually recommend a specific type to my boss, but my inclination is to go with ABC's because they've been around, they're in more companies, and they're more compatible industry-wide. Again, I don't know all that much about it. Maybe XYZ computers might be better because they have more education and training software. Right now, though, I think we should go for an in-house loop that would be ABC-compatible and would be compatible with the machines that we have in our district offices."

4.

SURVEYING

SURVEYING

By now the worst is over. You've checked any incipient writer's block by getting your first words down on paper. You've already come a long way! You've selected a topic, explored it in your mind, and scrawled what you know about it. That's more than most people do. Most just talk about what they're going to write. How many times have you heard people say, "Someday I'm going to write a book"? And how many even get close to starting? Until you commit something to paper and actually begin the writing process, nothing will happen—least of all a book manuscript. So, congratulations for getting farther than most. But what now? What do you do with your scores of discursive phrases, lists, and sentences?

The next step in the writing process is called *surveying*. Surveying requires just what it says: examining what you've written to find out what you know about the topic in order to learn what works, and to discover new connections.

Let's say you've just freewritten ten pages proposing that your company merge with XYZ Corporation. Many fellow employees would not even dare to think about such a wild idea, but you're just daring enough to write about it. OK. There they are on paper, the ramblings of a wild person; your thoughts are a jumble of words, phrases, and sentences that make sense to you alone. How do you refine your ideas so someone else can read and understand them, let alone accept and act on them? Surveying is the answer.

When you allow your ideas to flow wildly and creatively, you open the floodgates to torrents of possibilities. Unfortunately, you also allow lots of unnecessary words to wash in. Often only you can penetrate the wordiness; so, if you want others to understand and act on your ideas, you must clarify them. Surveying does that; it forces you to look over your fastwriting or scrawling for the big picture, for the developing trends—for the potential of your ideas.

Surveying is much like buying an older home as an investment. When you walk in the front door, it nearly falls off its hinges; the floors creak, and the banister dangles by a few screws. A lesser person might run, but the entrepreneur sees potential. Entrepreneurs notice the original oak doors, the sturdy maple banisters bolstered by bleached birch spindles, and the parquet floors. Why? Because when they survey that old house, they see its potential.

So how do you survey your writing for potential? Just like the entrepreneur does in that old house—by looking around and grouping things into categories. Most minds don't produce ideas in neat packages: ideas tend to free-float, waiting to connect with something in our lives or in our writing. In fact, that's what makes writing so much fun. It allows us to make new connections, ones we didn't know existed until we put them together on paper.

In this chapter you'll be introduced to the steps in surveying: reviewing what you've written, finding out what you know, deciding what works, discovering connections, and making a list of key words.

REVIEWING WHAT YOU'VE WRITTEN

A few hours or days after the fastwriting step, read through your draft quickly to get a sense of what you've written. By allowing time between fastwriting and surveying, your reading will be less subjective—much more objective and reader-like, less owner-like.

Now, read through the draft again, but this time ask yourself what ideas dominate the draft, what ideas can link with others? Many writers call the first scribbled draft a zero-base draft because its ideas lead directly to the first draft. Thus, the zero-base draft is an idea draft. Surveying helps you begin to organize and group your written ideas into an intelligible whole.

As you survey your draft for potential, use a yellow highlighter to underline ideas that seem to go together. The highlighter provides a broad "sweep" of the pen, which is exactly what you're looking for in this draft—sweeps of ideas.

Once you've swept through the draft, go back over and number or letter your ideas. For example, while sweeping through your draft, you might find an idea "A" on page one, with one related bit of information on page three, and yet another on page twelve. By lettering (or numbering) your ideas, you can locate and group apples with apples and oranges with oranges. This should help you decide how to construct your writing project.

For instance, you're writing about a new detergent that you think your laundry company should use. Let's look at how you might begin surveying. First, you've freewritten a memo to your boss about the advantages of switching detergents, and ended up with pages of fast-writing. Next, you go over your memo, high-lighter in hand, and on page two you discover your first good idea: the old product has increased in price by 13 percent over the last year. Label this idea "A." While proceeding with your survey, you see another idea: increased customer complaints about spots remaining in soiled shirts. Label this idea "B." Further on, you see that customers are com-plaining about the ten-cent increase in price for starching dress shirts—another "A" idea. As you proceed with your survey of the draft, you will discover that the labeled ideas will present you with a road map of where to go.

Remember: Most people don't think in nice straight lines, and your initial thoughts won't come out in neat categories. You need the sur-veying technique to help you recognize similar

ideas, so you can make organizational decisions.

What about the material you've left
unhighlighted? Forget it. It's extraneous, the
writer's equivalent to the film on the film
editor's cutting room floor. You must mentally
clip it off; forget it, and move on.

FINDING OUT WHAT
YOU KNOW

An immediate benefit of surveying is to
find out what you know about a topic.
Surveying, though sometimes humbling, can
often encourage you. Most of the time you will
finish your survey while saying to yourself,
"Great! I know a lot more than I thought about
widgets." By spreading the draft in front of you
and reviewing it for ideas, you gain confidence.

While surveying, you probably will find at
least one gaping hole in the middle of your
writing. For example, while surveying your
writing about new software for your company's computers, you discover the words
intercomputer compatibility, but you can only
highlight that phrase—there are no details.
You've just uncovered a good idea, but it

seems to need some research. In finding out what you don't know, you have given yourself a lead for the future.

DECIDING WHAT WORKS

At this point, you are making only temporary decisions. Surveying helps you tentatively decide what will work and what will not. Only when you've read what you've written can you decide what works or fails to work. Thinking and writing are close cousins, but they're not the same—no more so than writing and talking.

Remember, your thoughts may make perfect sense to you because you've got a particular mindset and base of information, but you can't assume they will make sense to your readers. You can't assume your readers know everything you do. Thus, you also have to assess the validity of the thoughts you put on paper. What "thinks" well does not necessarily "write" well, at least the first time; so, you need to survey.

While surveying, you might find some well-formed ideas, nearly perfect for reader consumption. Often these are old ideas that you've been refining and revising for years. However, you may also find germs of ideas, and these first-time thoughts are often ill-formed and imperfect. Such first-generation ideas, as opposed to tenth-generation thoughts, will require more scrutiny and revision.

Thus, you'll have to choose the ideas that will work the best. How good are the germ ideas? Are they worth more work, or are they just fleeting thoughts that should be left behind? Because you've written them down, you can focus on their individual worth, which is difficult to do when you're trying to hold a welter of ideas in your mind simultaneously.

DISCOVERING CONNECTIONS

Connections are as important in writing as they are in thinking. In Chapter 2 we looked at connections in the thinking stages of writing. Your mind constantly makes connections or associations: someone on the train reminds you of cousin Ed; a billboard advertising skin lotion shows a mountain scene, and you think of your trip to Vail last year. Your brain makes connections all the time, and through these connections you construct and view the world. It's the new connections you make between ideas that give life and vitality to your writing.

MAKING A LIST OF KEY WORDS

Finally, after you've highlighted the key ideas in your zero-base draft, list them on a separate piece of paper. If you put all the A's together, then all the B's, and so on, this list will become your working outline, your stepping-stone to the next stage of writing. Does that mean you must stick to this initial list? No. You'll revise this working outline as you continue to collect new ideas and information. It simply gives you a base on which to start adding new information or from which to slice away old, unworkable ideas.

Surveying forces you to review and account for what you've written, and to begin structuring your writing. Notice that before surveying you spent most of the time *producing* ideas. Now, you have practiced *choosing* among them.

Surveying gives you a beginning inventory of idea categories, and when you categorize them you can organize them, if only on a rudimentary level. From this point, you must decide how detailed you want to make the levels of your categories. This becomes the next step in the writing process: ***hunting***.

Your key idea list (outline) will help you with Hunting. You will use it as a shopping list when you turn to other sources. But it won't restrict you: if you find something you need in the store that's not on the list, you simply add it.

Writing Workshop #4
Surveying

Once you've gotten your thoughts about a topic on paper, you're ready to survey. Look for holes in your information—places in your fastwriting that seem to lack depth or substance. Surveying will help prepare you for the hunting phase.

Objectives

1. To clear away the clutter of the initial draft.

2. To discover what the writer does and does not know about the topic.

Activities

STEP 1
Review your discovery draft on a grand scale. Label similar groups of ideas with the same letter or number to help you establish how much information you have in each main category.

STEP 2

Review your groupings and list the areas that need more research or development.

STEP 3

Underline or highlight the key words in your draft. Also mark those words that seem essential or critically related to your topic.

STEP 4

Now, list your key words and phrases on a separate sheet of paper. This paper will be your working outline. A working outline is a mushy and flexible thing. It only gives tentative direction, so don't look at it as your final outline— don't think you have to stick with it. Quite the contrary: You'll revise your working outline constantly as you pore over the research.

Writing Illustration

NOTE: We'll use the freespeaking draft from Chapter 3 in this series of examples:

STEP 1: REVIEW THE DRAFT

Dear Joe,

I am a training coordinator for our company. This company is a large multinational ping-pong ball manufacturing company with a

substantial training center located in a subur-
ban area. My job is to ᴬ*teach communication
skills* to executives who will be going out to
the field for different reasons. In delivering our
programs to various executive groups it has
become evident that we are no longer capable
of doing as good a job as we could do with the
use of computers. I see the use of computers
enhancing my operation in several different
ways. We could also ᴮ*store* all of their lesson
plans on disks, which could then be available
to brand new instructors who come into my
group. Computers would give me a way of
measuring their performance and ᴬ*productivity*
in the year very quickly by reading out what
they have actually done. I could also use a
ᴮ*database system* to index a lot of the lesson
plans, and to index the various groups that we
teach for retrieval. This could be used for
reports that have to be done and for a variety
of purposes. This would really help my operation because it would ᴮ*eliminate file storage
problems*, eliminate a lot of need for hard copy,
and would give me and the instructors instant
retrieval when I or they need it. It would really
help the efficiency of the office. I can also use
the computer for ᶜ*scheduling*. My office needs
a lot of scheduling to keep it running efficiently. Right now it's being done by hand and

it's inefficient, and there are software packages out that could solve the whole problem. I could get a report on the status of anything I want, program progress in the office, and what we're doing. I also like the idea of using ^D***computer-based training*** (CBT) software to free up instructor time and enhance the trainee's experience. By using a CBT package, more students can receive more training with a ^D***decreased drain*** on instructors. Instructors, therefore, will have more time to give to those who need it. It's the ^E***kind of equipment*** that I don't know much about—the type of technical equipment out there or even how much it costs—but I do know there are ^E***ABC computers*** and ^E***XYZ computers*** available that I know something about, although I need to know more about the equipment and its capabilities before I can actually recommend a specific type to my boss. My inclination is to go with ABC because they're more compatible industry-wide. Again, I don't know all that much about it. Maybe XYZ computers might be better because they have more education and training software. Right now, though, I think we should go for an in-house loop that would be ^E***ABC-compatible*** and would be compatible with the machines that we have in our district offices.

STEP 2: LIST IDEAS NEEDING MORE RESEARCH
Kind of equipment
(Automated) scheduling systems
Database system
Computer-based training

STEP 3: HIGHLIGHT KEY WORDS
See emphasis in Step 2 example

STEP 4: LIST KEY WORDS
Training
Lesson plans
Database
Communication skills
Productivity
Scheduling system
ABC Computer Company
XYZ Computer Company
Performance
Storage
Retrieval
Costs

5.

HUNTING

HUNTING

In the previous chapter on surveying, you discovered what you do and do not know about your writing topic. Now you must take the time to close your knowledge gaps—to go *hunting*. If you were to ask someone where to go for information, what do you think most people, particularly students, would say? If you guessed the library or the company files, you're right, but they're wrong! You're right because that is what most students would say, but they're wrong because that's not the quickest way to begin the process of hunting for information.

In this chapter you will learn the hunting process: the way you can fill in gaps with information that will support your overall ideas. Specifically, you'll learn how to gather information from interviews, how to develop a thesis statement, where to find sources, how to "interview" a book or periodical, and how to take notes using notecards or notesheets.

INTERVIEWING OTHERS

By far the most overlooked, yet most helpful source of information is other people. In a sense, the process of hunting—whether for a company report, a school paper, or a civic club report—mirrors the modus operandi of a detective. Where do you begin? To answer this question you must first ask yourself what, in general, you want to know. If, for instance, you want to learn more about how to obtain computer technology for your new office, you need to think like a detective and to list on paper where you would find your most logical leads.

First, you might consider someone in your company who recently went through the same kind of search. Why reinvent the wheel? If someone else has done something similar to what you want to do, presumably that person had to go through the same steps you'd have to follow. He or she is likely to already have made all the false starts and mistakes along the way that you would make. Therefore, that person should be able to help you take the most direct route to success. In short, don't overlook human resources in favor of written ones.

Second, if you are a new employee, you may want to interview the person whose job you filled. Your predecessor can give you a valuable historical perspective. Remember, you should place a real premium on experience, and learning from that experience for the price of a phone call, even a long-distance one, is valuable.

Third, look to experts to guide your reading and tell you where to look next. Factory representatives, people in associations, and professionals can provide you with the kind of early direction you need as a writing detective. Covering some leads on the phone and others in person; listing and asking questions; and taking and transcribing good notes—all these things constitute the first big steps in hunting.

What do you get when you talk to an expert? You get information, both oral and written. For example, your "expert" may hand you a magazine article or two or even a book or Internet reference that contains the exact information you want. In other words, the person you've interviewed has already done some research for you—free of charge. You may, in fact, find all the answers you need in your first interview. But even if you don't, you will have more leads.

How do you question an expert? The best way is to state your interest and then begin with an open-ended question. For example: "I'm writing a proposal for new database applications for our corporate training office. Do you have any ideas or suggestions on the kind of equipment or requirements I should look for?" This kind of a wide-open question should induce any expert to wax eloquently, which in turn will lead you to other questions. By starting with broad questions, you'll stimulate a relaxed and free-flowing dialogue. From there you'll find the interviewing process a natural one.

Before you get right into questioning your experts, however, you must establish a degree of rapport with them—you have to earn the right to ask them a question. This is a ritual in all societies. If you walk up to a total stranger on your commuter train and begin asking a series of questions about anything except the time, your chances of being rebuffed are high. However, if you strike up a friendly, low-key discussion about the commute, you can then gradually discuss where you work and what you do. Eventually your commuting acquaintance may allow you to ask more probing questions.

The same holds true when you talk to experts. Introduce yourself and tell them what you want to do. If you expect their help, you must first give them information. Tell them why you came to them, and they'll start off being flattered. If you believe that these people know their stuff, tell them so. You'll immediately score points and open the door to discussion.

One interview may lead to several others, and after a short time you can focus on a particular idea. Turning this idea into words early on makes hunting and subsequent writing much easier.

DEVELOPING A THESIS STATEMENT

Purpose gives direction to your work and life. If you decide to run in marathons, you'll immediately begin to run progressively more miles, get more sleep, improve your eating habits, and perhaps read running magazines. Your decision to run in marathons gives you direction. In writing, it is the same: You must develop a central focus (or thesis, as it's called in writing) to set you on your hunting path.

Let's say your initial idea was simply **computers**. Without focus, your hunt would involve interviewing thousands of people and reading hundreds, maybe even thousands, of books and periodicals, not to mention scouring Internet material. Who knows if you'd ever get anywhere. Your focus would be considerably narrowed if you had chosen "computers at work," though this, too, is still a very rough idea. In hunting for your thesis, you'd no longer need to worry about video games or home applications—you'd eliminate much of your research.

If you can refine your search to a single focus, you'll have developed a thesis statement and will be well on the way to successful hunting. You might try as a potential thesis statement: "Certain personal computer applications in the training office would make the office more effective and efficient." Can you see how this statement makes your purpose more direct and clear than the initial one of computers? You've merely narrowed the focus.

To refine your ideas and develop your thesis statement, you should ask yourself: "What am I trying to do (or to prove) in this piece of writing?" If you find it difficult to write a developed thesis, try talking it out with someone—rehearse your purpose. Indeed, some people come to writing through oral communication. As you explain your paper to a friend or spouse, you'll begin to connect your ideas, which will help you put them into a single provable statement: your thesis statement.

Does this mean that you can't change this newly developed thesis statement? No. You'll revise this one as you learn new information, but eventually you will find a statement that exactly suits your purpose. Also, when you begin hunting, don't worry if you're not sure what you're looking for. Most writers start off blindly, discovering their path along the way. So, you can begin interviewing with only a mini-thesis in mind. The sooner you develop your specific point of focus, however, the more efficiently you will be able to interview, and the faster your writing will go.

WHERE TO FIND SOURCES

Once you've talked with the people who can help you in your quest, turn to institutions. You will find sources located in companies, associations, and libraries.

Never, for example, neglect the institutional knowledge you can find stored away in company files. Depending on the extent and comprehensiveness of your organization's filing systems, you may find all the information you need tucked safely away in company files. Why not see what the institution already has to offer?

Second, consider associations. There are thousands of associations in Washington, D.C., the headquarters of many organizations. Associations representing everything from car dealers to concrete manufacturers store vast amounts of specialized industry-related data. For example, the National Association of Broadcasters houses a fine library, chock full of data on the industry, and it is a necessary stop for anyone writing about the media. Many associations have their own home pages.

Third and most familiar is the institution we call the library. Eventually, we all end up there because it is an invaluable resource. Although neither this chapter nor this book will turn you into a research expert, make sure you consider the following library resources: the electronic card catalogue, the reader's guides to periodical literature, and the research librarians.

The electronic card catalogue lists the library's collection of books in three primary ways, but you may search under any field held in the database: by title, by author, and by subject. Thus, *The Computer in Business* by John Doe could be found either under *Computer in Business, The* (its title); Doe, John (its author); or computer business (its subject). A quick search through the subject catalogue, which is automated in most libraries, will give you a good general idea of what your library has available in your topic area. Often you can establish your bedrock research by stopping here first.

Because the cycle of book publication often takes two years, you'll have to turn to periodicals and newspapers for current information. Most libraries have a periodical room for you to find out the most up-to-date information. Here you'll discover a myriad of indexes: *The Social Science Index, The Business Index, The Criminal Justice Periodical Index, The Reader's Guide to Periodical Literature*, and an array of others, including newspaper indexes (*The New York Times, The Washington Post,* etc.). Indeed, libraries now have many of these indexes on computer, giving you direct access to them with the touch of a keyboard. Though each index presents its information differently, all are arranged, at the least, by topic. Thus, by searching appropriate indexes you can usually substantially update your research.

Of course, another key research tool is the Internet. It's like having a world resource at your fingertips. By using any one of a number of search engines, you can mine for gold. However, some sites are put up by individuals whose research and credibility may not be tested. Stick with known names and companies or organizations for the most reliability.

Finally, never overlook the librarians, especially the research librarians. They can help you find almost anything, while introducing you to resources you've never imagined. If you expect to research and write on a regular basis, be sure to establish a friendly working relationship with the research librarians at the outset. You will earn their respect early on by doing your homework before talking to them. That is, before you ask a question, make sure you've already tried to solve the problem yourself. Always tell the librarians that you've checked this, that, and then this other thing—all to no avail. They will then know you're not using them as a card catalogue and usually will go out of their way to help a fellow researcher. By doing your homework, you automatically build a bond of respect and trust with librarians.

INTERVIEWING DOCUMENTS

Most of us interview other people simply by talking with them. We do it every day—at work, at home, and in social settings. Gleaning information from others is nothing new. "How are you?" "What's new?" "How many days will it take to deliver?" But when it comes to using books and other documents, some people get nervous.

And they shouldn't. After all, a document is pretty much mute, until you know how to get it talking. Start by asking it a few easy questions!

A book, for example. The title page alone gives you a lot of information: along with telling you what's inside the book, it gives you the title, the author, the place of publication, and the publisher.

Second, the book itself provides at least one—and often two—excellent "finder" mechanisms: the Table of Contents and the Index. Skim the Table of Contents first to see if the book covers your area of interest, and also to see if you may have overlooked any related items. Next, scan the Index in the back of the book. Most lengthy manuscripts include indexes that help you quickly locate specific subtopics; a quick scan can tell you whether you want to check out the book or put it back in the stacks.

Once you've decided that you want to use a book or periodical, you've got to record your "interview." Many people have a hard time developing a systematic method to record information and research. Why not consider what many professional writers do: recording their sources, and using notecards, notesheets, or photocopies. First, we'll look at making bibliography cards, then at making notecards.

Bibliography Cards

You need a system to record both the books and periodicals you've used and the people you've interviewed so you can readily refer back to them. Use either a notecard (either paper or electronic) or a notesheet to

record the pertinent data: title, author, date
and place of publication, edition number, publisher, and page numbers if it's a periodical.
Also, for your own help, record the book's call
sign and the library you found it in, especially if
you plan to use several libraries. Alternatively,
you can photocopy the title page, along with
the table of contents, index, or both. This
method is much quicker and often more com-
prehensive.

Next, number each bibliography card or
page consecutively (that is, label the first book
you reviewed number one, and so on). Thus,
each resource will have a unique identifier for
you to use when you begin taking notes.
Remember to keep your bibliography cards or
sheets separate from your notes so you can
control your data.

Notecards and Notesheets

Collecting information from books, periodicals, and even interviews and having it easily
available later is easy if you set up a system
ahead of time. Disorder early in the research
process leads to late confusion and dismay in
your writing. You can avoid frustration by
employing a simple, time-tested system of

information handling: the systematic use of notecards or notesheets. Specifically, you should produce a notecard or notesheet for every piece of information or idea you find worthy of recording. This section will explain how to use a slug line, how to paraphrase (and why you should), and what other information to include on the card.

First, create a slug line. When you record information on any notecard, always summarize the contents of your source in a single, short synopsis sentence, just like a headline. For example: "Computers save work, money, and time." Put this slug at the top of a card, **then** go on to explore the views of your expert (or book). The slug line gives you a quick reference and synopsis so that weeks or months later when you are ready to write, you can sort your cards without having to read the entire entry. Slug lines are great time-savers.

Second, when possible, paraphrase the information you collect. Long, involved quotes strung together look like artificial fillers, the product of a writer too lazy to assimilate and interpret the data. Even more disturbing, the patchwork of multiple styles that results from too many direct quotes will give your writing the Frankenstein effect—your writing won't be **yours**.

On the other hand, when you paraphrase, you learn and assimilate knowledge—a major purpose of writing. Your writing will sound like you wrote it, not someone else. With only one owner, your writing also carries an even, clear tone—something readers really appreciate. Remember, if you do have to quote someone because the language is so good or the corroboration from a noteworthy source is pertinent, make the quotes short and sweet. Avoid long block quotes.

Third, always record specific location information on each card. Remember to include the number you have assigned on the information's bibliography card. Many people put this number in a circle in the upper right-hand corner. Next, write the slug line at the top of the card, and underline it for emphasis. And make sure you include the source's page number for future reference and footnoting purposes. Once you've completed the notecard, file it away. Before long, you'll begin to see patterns developing in your notes that later will become useful when you prepare to write.

SYSTEMATIC PROCESS

Hunting is a small part of the writing process itself. First, you begin with what you know—your writing draft. Next, you interview people who know the subject—experienced others and experts. Through open-ended questions, they can provide you with productive leads to follow up on that can save you enormous amounts of time. With information in hand, develop your thesis—the statement you propose to prove in your writing. Your thesis will be a guiding light for you and the reader. With thesis in hand, head for companies, associations, and libraries to find more sources of information.

Use notecards or notesheets to record information. Don't forget the critical identification information on each card, and pay attention to accuracy and detail. By having a systematic method to take notes from your sources, you will make your research a much more manageable process.

Use these steps in the hunting process and your work will be more systematic and, in the end, easier.

Writing Workshop #5
Hunting

Now that you've completed your survey, you're ready to begin filling in the holes—the gaps you may have found in your writing. To make the job of filling those holes easier, follow these steps in the process called Hunting.

Objectives

1. To record relevant information from resources.

2. To collect sufficient information for your piece of writing.

Activities

STEP 1

Interview people who know about your topic. Find an expert or two and get some leads before you go to the library.

STEP 2

Review your notes and interviews, and try to write one sentence that focuses your thoughts on the topic—your thesis sentence. To help, finish this sentence: ***In this paper I will prove that*** _____. A thesis sentence tells you and the reader what you'll support with your research and writing.

STEP 3

With your thesis statement and some leads in mind, go to company files and documents and to the library (corporate, public, etc.). Use the electronic card catalogue, the magazine guides, any available databases, the Internet, and government documents to formulate a working bibliography. Like the working outline, this bibliography represents your best guess at references that might work well for your project. This tentative list will be subject to additions and deletions, so keep an open mind.

STEP 4

Begin taking notes. Develop a slug line for each card that matches your working outline. Paraphrase the source in your own words. If a new but important topic appears, add a new line to the outline. Next, add the bibliographic reference and page number.

Writing Illustration

STEP 1: INTERVIEWING EXPERTS

I chose to interview our computer expert, Mary Jane Byte. She explained that we already have a file in our company records about the application of computers to training. Further, she indicated that I should look at the brochures she has on Company XYZ because they contain an example relevant to my project. Finally, she referred me to an *ORD Computer* magazine article dated January 1997 entitled "Modernizing the Training Process," by Blume and Sollie. She also agreed to look over my draft later to make sure I didn't misinterpret anything. The interview took 20 minutes and headed me in the right direction.

STEP 2: WRITING A THESIS SENTENCE

In this memo I will prove that computers can improve my training operation.

STEP 3: DEVELOPING A WORKING BIBLIOGRAPHY

Source 1: Interview with Mary Jane Byte, company computer coordinator, conducted January 17, 1998.

Source 2: Article entitled "Modernizing the Training Process," by Blume and Sollie, in ***ORD Computer*** magazine, dated January 1997.

Source 3: Company files entitled, "Computer Applications," file # Computer-143514.

STEP 4: TAKING NOTES

Bibliography Cards

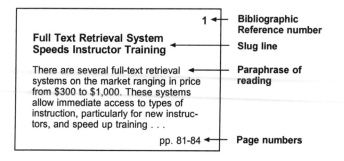

Bibliographic Reference number — 1

Slug line — Full Text Retrieval System Speeds Instructor Training

Paraphrase of reading — There are several full-text retrieval systems on the market ranging in price from $300 to $1,000. These systems allow immediate access to types of instruction, particularly for new instructors, and speed up training . . .

Page numbers — pp. 81-84

6.

WRITING

WRITING

Early in the writing process you did some writing, remember? You freewrote or free-spoke—fastwriting techniques that help you get your ideas on paper quickly—to find out what you knew about your topic. Well, now you're going to do it all over again, only this time with the benefit of some notes on what you learned from others about the topic. This step of the writing process integrates what you know already with the information you've learned while hunting. In this chapter you'll learn how to organize your notes, how to use your preliminary outline, how to refine your thesis, and how to write freely with new information.

ORGANIZING YOUR NOTES

In the Hunting step you tested the waters of opinion and knowledge: you found out what others had to say about your topic. No doubt you've accumulated a pile of notecards or notesheets for your efforts. So now what? Well, now you need to sort out the information so you can use it wisely in a draft.

Begin by reading each of your slug lines and placing each card in a specific pile. Remember that key-word list you made, that tentative outline of ideas? Now is a good time to retrieve that list and review each word for its potential as an outline heading. Use this list to create the categories for your card piles. When you come to a card that doesn't fit into any existing categories, add a new category to your list. You're starting to flesh out the outline. Now you're ready for the next step.

Thoroughly reread each of the cards in the particular categories. After that, read them again. Most people require three to four readings to master the information, and that's what the writing step is all about: the mastery and assimilation of information.

As already mentioned, when you read each card and check it against your rough, key-word outline, you'll find yourself revising the outline by adding and deleting key words. Remember, outlines are always evolving: as you learn more, you refine them more.

At this point, after you have reviewed your notes extensively, a few things will occur. First, you'll realize that you've collected some irrelevant information. Invariably, as you cast a wide net to catch information, you'll take in more fish than you'll ever need. So, throw them back. Just put the notes in a file and save them, or use them to start a new fire next winter. You might toss out as much as 50 percent of your notes. Remember, the purpose of research is to determine what's out there, and then to collect it. When you begin a quest, you're not at all sure what you'll need, so you collect everything. But once you begin paring it down, you should look critically at what you can and cannot use.

Next, you'll note that your rough, key-word outline needs some fine tuning—one of the purposes of the writing step. New words and ideas will begin finding their way into your writing. You'll go back and forth from your notes to your working outline, and soon you'll arrive at a very rough outline or map of your writing project. You don't need to have a fully formed plan to write your draft. However, some people prefer to produce an exact outline during this step. We will examine the form for a final outline in the next chapter, so, for now, let's assume you will stick to your working outline.

Now, with assimilated notes in hand, you've got an outline that gives a general direction to your upcoming draft. But before you begin, you need a clearer vision of where you're going. The best way to get that is to develop a more concise thesis statement.

REFINING THE THESIS STATEMENT

Remember when you developed a rough thesis statement to help your hunting? Now it's time to refine that statement, if you haven't already done so. Having thoroughly read all of your notecards, you should be in a good position to refine your statement based on the additional information.

First, read your notes once more. Then, sit back and pretend you're talking to a friend. The friend should be an "intelligent ignorant"—a well-read, interested, and ready listener who happens to know very little about your topic. You may even find it useful to make a tape recording of your imaginary conversation. Tell her or him what your writing project is all about. Try to reduce the topic to a single thesis sentence—the point you want to support with the evidence you've collected.

Why is a thesis so important? Because it directs and limits what you include in your paper. If, for example, your thesis reads "Computers in training offices require a wide range of software," your development of that thesis will be much different from one that states, "Computers in training save teachers time and increase their productivity." Both of these theses revolve around computers in training, yet they will produce two very different papers. Notice that when you develop a clear thesis, it is easier to write a draft.

WRITING THE DRAFT

Now comes the fun part: writing. You need only refer to Chapter 4 for the fastwriting techniques: freewriting, freelisting, webbing, and freespeaking. To create a full-text draft immediately, you should use either freewriting or freespeaking. You must eventually convert the other two systems to a text; thus, they add another step to your process.

When you freewrite or freespeak, be careful to keep going, even if your words still need polishing. Keep pushing forward and, if possible, avoid reading your cards. Of course, you can refer to your notes, but to give your draft a fresh and natural tone, try to do this sparingly.

Also, try to produce this working draft as quickly as you can, with as few interruptions as possible. Keep the flow going; get the draft out so you'll have something to work with. Once you've completed the draft, put it down for a day or two to get some distance from it. Remember, time can work for you as long as you don't allow it to turn into procrastination. Time lets you review the draft with fresh eyes.

REVIEWING THE DRAFT

When you read through your draft, you will find some holes. Some of the holes you'll be able to fill immediately, and some you won't.

First, you'll find information you left out, because you forgot it or had trouble explaining it. Perhaps, for example, you were writing your draft on computerizing the training office, and when you got to computerizing lesson plans you got a phone call and lost your train of thought. Now, with a clear mind, you should be able to spot this gaping hole and plug it in immediately.

Second, holes can and do occur, not just because of oversight, but because of **under-thought**. In such cases, you will have to review your notes and perhaps return to the library or a specific source for more information. Or you simply may have to take more time rereading your notes, in order to truly assimilate the information you've already collected.

This step in the writing process produces the first draft. Now you have something you can mold—add to and take away from. You've taken a big step toward completing your writing by producing this draft, and you'll be amazed at how fast you complete the remaining steps.

Writing Workshop #6
Writing

Now that you've done some research and collected some hard facts, you're ready to write a first draft. How do you start? It's easy. Just go back to your favorite fastwriting style.

Objectives

1. To organize and sort resource cards.

2. To develop a consistent voice throughout the paper.

Activities

STEP 1

Review all of your notecards and match them to your working outline. Revise the outline where necessary. Share your outline with your writing process partner for feedback.

STEP 2

After reviewing your notes, refine your thesis statement. Talk to a hypothetical "intelligent ignorant," explaining in one sentence what you hope to develop in your own piece of writing.

STEP 3

Review your cards again and set aside any that don't fit your thesis. Don't throw them away, because you might change your mind later.

STEP 4

Study your notes intensely. Describe the substance of your report to your partner.

STEP 5

Now you are ready to write your first draft. Put your notes away. As fast as you can, freespeak or freewrite, based on what you remember from the notes and common knowledge. Again, don't worry about spelling or mechanics; just let the words fly.

Writing Illustration

STEP 1: REVISING THE OUTLINE

After reviewing my notecards, I made the following revision to my initial working outline. I added *quick-find*, a system that allows full text retrieval; *full check*, a program that checks the spelling of word processing; *hard disk*, for increased storage; and *screen covers*, which reduce screen glare for users.

Training
Lesson plans
Database
Communication skills
Productivity
Scheduling system
ABC Computer Company
XYZ Computer Company
Performance
Storage
Retrieval
Costs
Quick-find
Full check
Hard disk
Screen covers

STEP 2: REFINING THE THESIS STATEMENT

In this memo I hope to prove that the effectiveness and efficiency of communications training can be significantly improved through the use of computers.

STEP 3: REVIEWING THE NOTECARDS

I went through my cards and found out that I had to toss out about 30 percent of the cards that I had gathered. I had gathered about 60 cards, and I put 18 aside.

STEP 4: STUDYING THE NOTES

I spent about an hour or so reviewing my cards before beginning Step 5.

STEP 5: FREEWRITING THE FIRST DRAFT

Here is the freewriting draft I wrote:

Teaching communications to executives of a multinational ping-pong ball manufacturing company is my job. In delivering communication packages to executive groups, it has become clear to me that we need to become more effective and efficient.

One real problem in the office is not having some form of an index and a retrieval system for lesson plans. Through research in **ORD Computer** magazine, I discovered a system that is now available for $900 called "Quick-Find." Quick-Find allows full text retrieval in an indexing system that will give ready access to any disk data. So, whenever anyone new comes into the office, he or she will be able, with a series of commands, to pull up any information he or she needs based on indexing commands. For example, if instructors want to know what is on file concerning nonverbal communications, they can enter the words **nonverbal communication** on the command line, and all the information will be pulled up from the stored lesson plans. A computer can also serve as a scheduler for the office.

My office also requires an enormous amount of scheduling because our training takes place on demand and at both on-site and off-site locations. According to **Computer Match** magazine, "Schedule Master" ($600)—a software package that is available—will meet our company's needs. This program will be able to track all of our appointments and schedules as well as all of our communications that are incoming and outgoing, so that we can track when we send information out on our processors.

Computer-based training (CBT) software is also available to free up instructor time and enhance the trainee's experience. According to Stallbach (1997), drill and practice exercises using a computer in the classroom increase the efficiency of the trainer by at least 25 percent. By using a CBT package, the instructor is relieved of purely mechanical responsibilities and can devote time to more vital training.

Two packages are available that review the fundamentals of speech as well as provide drill and practice exercises. They cost $500 each and are available from the Real-Time Computer Software Company.

Regarding PC's, I've looked specifically at ABC computers and XYZ computers and found that because the ABC computers are the most widespread in industry and have the greatest amount of business software, their likely suitability over the long run seems to be far greater than any other, even though they are more expensive. I estimate we will need five

PC's: one for secretarial/typing support, two on remote-independent stations for instructors' use, one at my desk for management control, and one as a server for our network. The estimated cost for hardware and software is less than $25,000.

7.

REVISING

REVISING

You've finally gotten your ideas and research down in writing. Sure, your draft isn't the prettiest piece of polished writing you've ever seen, but remember, you've conquered the toughest part: getting your topic on paper. The next few steps go quickly because you can work with a concrete piece of writing.

Now it's time to take the writing that makes sense to you and fashion it to make sense to others: your readers. The revising step marks a shift in your writing process. You shift your concern from producing your ideas to communicating those ideas to others. In a sense, you shift from being author-centered to being reader-centered.

In this chapter you'll look at how to make your writing understandable to readers through well-constructed paragraphs. You will learn to scan your draft for related ideas, develop topic sentences, create unity with transitions, and watch paragraph length. In short, you'll learn how to write effective paragraphs.

SCANNING THE DRAFT

The first revising activity for writing effective paragraphs is to scan your entire draft quickly and look for related ideas. You'll find that in early freewriting you scatter your ideas more than in the latter stages of writing. This phenomenon is easily explained.

In the beginning, your mind has trouble focusing; thus, your thoughts start, stop, and shift. But once you get started, your thinking and, consequently, your writing seem to settle down into more logical grooves. Some professors tell their students to tear off the first page of their papers before turning in the remaining pages to them. These instructors have discovered that the first page is usually full of unnecessary writing, and they see little sense in reading it.

So, review your draft. A lettering system of A, B, C, D or a numbering system of 1, 2, 3, 4, 5 will help you label similar ideas in your draft. Remember to put apples with apples and oranges with oranges. This first revising step is macroscopic: you want to get an overall logical grouping of ideas.

Now that you've labeled similar ideas, move them closer to each other. Cutting and pasting on the computer works just fine. If you use a colored pencil, simply draw arrows. If the movement requires a major shift, you might do well to rearrange sheets of paper or notecards, just as you did when hunting. Sheets or cards are simple but effective organizing tools of the trade. By listing the related ideas on a single document, you'll be able to concentrate on the related ideas as a whole.

Having done that, you're ready for a second organizing principle: the topic sentence.

DEVELOPING TOPIC SENTENCES

When you review each of your idea groupings—particularly if you've put nearly identical ideas together—you'll see patterns develop. For example, if you're writing about computers in the work setting, you may find a group of sentences dealing with the efficiency of computers: "Computers allow quick revisions requiring little effort." "Computers store enormous amounts of data in small amounts of space." "Computers permit even the novice typist to produce near-perfect drafts

through revision." When you step back from
these related statements, you can see a pat-
tern evolving: they all deal with computer
efficiency. Now, write a single sentence to
encapsulate the general theme of this group of
sentences. You might write: "Computers are
efficient in a work setting." By writing this
overview statement, you've just written a topic
sentence for a paragraph. Easy enough?

Where should you place the topic sentence
in a paragraph? Theoretically, you can put it
anywhere. Realistically, you should write it at
the beginning of the paragraph to provide a
forecast of coming events. What else does the
topic sentence do for your readers? It gives
them a conceptual overview of what follows: It
offers a preview of coming attractions. The
topic sentence tells readers what to expect
and, at the same time, hints at the facts that
follow. For example:

*It takes very few seconds to perform
this function. It is a multi-stepped
operation that necessitates dexterity.
The individual with keen motor development can accomplish it with relative
ease, and the results are startling,
immediate, and rewarding. Most of all,*

*it's a healthy, cheap, and simple way
to ensure a relatively germ-free
society.*

What's this paragraph about? Without a topic sentence up front to give you an overview, it is difficult, if not impossible, to understand. This paragraph's topic sentence might well be: "Washing your hands is a step-by-step process that can prevent germs." Now reread the paragraph, and undoubtedly it will make more sense to you. Why? Because you had some idea about its objective before you got the details. So now you know how the topic sentence operates. We learn particulars more easily when they follow a general overview or framework.

Think about how difficult it is when a child or a friend runs up to you and gives you a series of facts with no reference: "He's bleeding, the street's a mess, John's crying, it's not my fault." Though you may be able to piece this one together, you usually have to ask, "What's this all about?" Then you get a topic sentence like "John fell off his bike." Now the facts (bleeding, crying, etc.) make sense, because you can fit them into an overall framework.

Again, to develop a topic sentence (1) review your related sentences, and (2) write out a sentence that summarizes them. Remember, the sentences following your topic sentence should support and prove it. They must relate directly back to the topic sentence. Keep apples with apples—don't mix. If in one paragraph you talk about a computer's efficiency in the work setting, don't wander off into its recreational uses. Save that for another paragraph, maybe even another chapter.

MAKING TRANSITIONS

Just as topic sentences *unify* the whole paragraph (give overall meaning to its facts), transition sentences *organize* the pieces of writing within the paragraph. Thus, writing can be unified but still be disorganized. Even as they travel down a well-developed topic sentence, the readers need some road signs or transitions. Devices such as conjunctions, pronouns, repeated words, and synonyms provide these road signs. In this section, you'll learn how transitions can help your writing and your readers.

The role of a writer is much like that of a tour guide. Your readers trail right behind you: All look to see what you point out, and all follow you with at least moderate attention. However, if you give a false direction or no direction at all, you'll miscue your pack of interested followers and sometimes even lose them.

CONJUNCTIONS

Conjunctions are just one way of keeping readers on track. You may know where you're going, but your readers won't, unless you give them a hint. So, words such as *and, but, as, as well as, also, however, therefore, thus, further,* and *moreover*, as well as directive phrases such as *in contrast, on the other hand*, and *in other words*, all depict the relationship of one part of your writing to another.

To illustrate, if you write, "Computers are useful in the office setting, but . . .," the reader has a clue from the word **but** that what follows will oppose or contrast what you've just said. On the other hand (see how this phrase will work on you as a reader), if you were to say, "Computers are useful in the office setting. Therefore . . ." your reader expects you to draw a conclusion, because words like **thus** and **therefore** imply a conclusion. Thus (see, there it is again!), by using specific transitional words you can cue your readers and keep them on track. Remember, transitions help readers understand relationships. The following list will help you with transitions:

Relationship	*Transition*
addition	also, and, moreover, further, similarly, likewise
comparison	in the same way, likewise
opposition/contrast	but, however, on the other hand, yet
example	for example, for instance
cause and effect	as a result, thus, therefore, hence
time and/or space	above, around, earlier, soon, then
summary	at last, finally, in conclusion, in summary

Transitions serve as the signposts that help readers stay with you. If you shift directions, give them a hint—an inclination of your new direction. They'll appreciate your help and reward you by reading on, instead of discarding your writing for something less frustrating.

PRONOUNS

One simple method of offering transitions in your writing is to use pronouns. Pronouns are stand-ins (they substitute for nouns) that refer back to your subject: thus, they provide a link—a transition. If you say, "Computer research indicates high usage in the daytime. *It* also indicates . . .," the reader knows that it refers back to *computer research*. You've provided transition without any boring repetition. However, use caution with your pronouns. Make sure they enhance clarity rather than confuse your meaning. For example: "John and Mark stopped by the gym, and then *he* stopped to make a call." It's impossible for the reader to know exactly who "he" refers to in this sentence. Be careful how, when, and where you place pronouns. Keep them close to their nouns, and if any possibility of confusion exists, restate the noun or start a new sentence: "John and Mark stopped by the gym, and then *Mark* stopped to make a call."

REPEATED WORDS AND SYNONYMS

As a final method of transition in your paragraphs, try either repeating a word from one sentence to another or using a synonym. Both of these techniques keep the flow of the paragraph going.

To illustrate, read the following:

Our company's president entered the room and sat down at the conference table to begin the meeting. We had called this meeting to discuss the purchase of several new products that would increase the efficiency of the office. Routinely, we scheduled all such conferences in the morning because the boss was happiest then.

Notice how the writer used *meeting* in the first sentence and then repeated it in the next to keep up the flow. But in sentence three, the writer substituted *conference* for *meeting*. Also, see how the synonym *boss* in the last sentence gets us back to the *company's president* in a way that fits the tone of the sentence. The paragraph flows because of transitional elements and repetition, and the use of synonyms.

PARAGRAPH LENGTH

How long should you make your paragraphs? Some might say, "As long as they need to be." But such an answer, while theoretically correct, gives little practical help to the people asking the question. As a general guide, try to keep your sentence length to two or three typed lines. Make paragraphs three to five sentences long—about 75 to 125 words.

In easy-to-remember terms, when you look at a double-spaced typed page, it ought to have at least two paragraphs per page. Why? Because paragraphs are meant to focus on *one* thought, not several. Second, they are intended to be breaks or resting stops for readers. When paragraphs get too long or involved, they violate both of these intentions. Long, involved paragraphs become tedious and confusing to readers, breaking their concentration and causing them to lose interest.

COMMUNICATING
YOUR IDEAS

Paragraphs are designed for readers, not writers. They encourage a reader's understanding and come at a time in the writing process when you, as a writer, must shift from idea **production**—getting your ideas down on paper—to idea **communication**. You must now direct that communication to your readers.

Readers need your help. Remember, **you** know what you're saying, but your readers do not. Help them by developing sound, well-written paragraphs. Use clearly designed topic sentences, and weave transitional elements into each paragraph so readers can easily follow the development of your ideas. If communication is the objective of writing, understanding is paramount, and paragraph development essential.

Writing Workshop #7
Revising

In your first draft, you have produced ideas that are invaluable to your writing. But those ideas often are jumbled and unrefined—raw material really. The initial editing process, Revising, helps you put apples with apples. It helps you organize your ideas into coherent paragraphs for future, more refined drafts.

Objectives

1. To organize ideas.

2. To develop internal unity within paragraphs.

Activities

STEP 1

Go through your writing draft quickly and group similar ideas. Label these ideas with A, B, C, etc.; 1, 2, 3, etc.; or with color codes from colored pencils. Any device will do, as long as it groups similar ideas. Remember, don't put apples with oranges: apples go with other apples and oranges with other oranges.

STEP 2

Now group the ideas into paragraphs of three to five sentences. Longer or shorter ones can cause comprehension difficulties for the reader. Look at your grouped sentences and come up with one sentence that sums up the paragraph. This sentence, your topic sentence, will introduce the paragraph by giving the reader an overview of what follows.

STEP 3

Look for ways to link the paragraphs so they flow naturally from one to another—a technique called transition. Repeat one of the last words of one paragraph in the topic sentence of the next. Use pronouns that refer back to a previous sentence or use connectives like ***and, but, however, also, further,*** and ***moreover***.

Writing Illustration

STEP 1: REGROUPING IDEAS

NOTE: I've labeled, grouped, and initially paragraphed a version of my draft from Chapter 6. It's still rough, but like ideas are together and are easier to work with:

Teaching communications to executives of a multinational ping-pong ball manufacturing company is my job. In delivering communication packages to executive groups, it is clear to me that we need to become more effective and efficient.

New instructors need access to lesson plans on file for efficiency. Our old word-of-mouth system is not effective. In the office we don't have any form of an [A]*indexing*/retrieval system for lesson plans.

There is inexpensive indexing/retrieval software that will help new instructors. Through research in **ORD Computer** magazine, I discovered a system that is now available for $900 called "Quick-Find." Quick-Find allows full-text retrieval in an [A]*indexing system* that will give ready access to any disk data. So whenever anyone new comes into the office, he or she will be able, using a series of commands, to pull up any information he or she needs based on [A]*indexing* commands. For example, if instructors want to know what is on file concerning nonverbal communications, they can enter the words **nonverbal communication** on the command line, and all the information will be pulled up from the stored lesson plans.

A computer can serve as a [B]*scheduler* for the office. My office also requires an enormous amount of scheduling because our training takes place on demand and at both on-site and off-site locations. According to ***Computer Match*** magazine, "Schedule Master" ($600)—a software package that is available—can meet our company's needs. This program will be able to track all of our appointments and [B]*schedules* as well as all of our communications that are incoming and outgoing so that we can track when we send information out on our processors.

Regarding PC's, I've looked specifically at ***ABC computers*** and ***XYZ computers*** and found that because the ABC computers are the most widespread in industry and have the greatest amount of business software, even though they are more expensive, their likely suitability over the long run seems to be far greater than any other. I estimate we will need five PC's: one for secretarial/typing support, two on remote-independent stations for instructors' use, one at my desk for management control, and one as a server. The estimated cost for hardware and software is less than $25,000.

STEP 2: WRITING THE TOPIC SENTENCE

What follows is a typical topic sentence and paragraph:

> *Teaching of communications breaks down into two general areas: writing communication skills and public speaking communication skills. Both of these skills are "doing skills." They require hands-on training as well as drill-and-practice training. Instruction in both skills sets can be enhanced by computer-based training.*

STEP 3: LINK THE PARAGRAPHS

Below is an example of a transition:

> *Computer-based training can also "transition word" free up instructor*

time. According to Stallbach (1997), drill and practice exercises using a computer in the classroom increase the efficiency of the trainer by at least 25 percent. By using a CBT package, the instructor is relieved of purely mechanical responsibilities and can devote time to more vital training.

8.

REWRITING

REWRITING

Buildings, automobiles, and virtually all objects have some type of structure to give them form. Written documents are no different. Certain structural conventions, if followed, give any document the form it needs to stand on its own.

Any well-constructed document contains three major structural elements: the introduction, the body, and the conclusion. This chapter will explore all three elements in detail, as well as show how they become the overall structure of any organized piece of writing.

Regardless of what you write, this format—introduction, body, conclusion—provides a basic structure. For example, a memo, though short, contains an introduction (usually the reference or purpose line) that states the thesis of the memorandum. This thesis or controlling topical sentence gives the reader the direction and scope of the memorandum. Longer memorandum reports are also commonly found in business and government. These reports usually contain a summary or executive summary paragraph right in the beginning, before the details. Longer reports, ranging from 20 to 50 pages, have an introductory section that, among other things, explains specialized vocabulary used in the report. Further, they feature an abstract of the key topic sentences in the document, in addition to the index. For book-length documents, an introductory chapter is appropriate. Such a chapter provides topical and structural guidance to the reader. Thus, the longer the document, the more structure it needs to help the reader.

Structure is intended for readers, not for writers. Writers understand what they write about; it is structure that conveys these ideas to readers. All structure seems to have this general format: the introduction, the body, and the conclusion. You should allow 15 percent of the total document length for the introduction, 75 percent for the body, and 10 percent for the conclusion.

THE INTRODUCTION

Let's begin with the introduction. First, you need to get your reader's attention. Generally, you are in competition for a reader's time. So, when creating a document, such as a memo, a report, or whatever, try to begin with a startling statistic or idea that will draw attention to your topic. A statistic that makes the reader say, "Wow, I didn't know this!" works particularly well. A second method might begin with several rhetorical questions. One question can be effective, two or three seem to have more impact on the reader; more than three questions becomes tedious. Third, you might begin with some sort of a short story, something brief and illustrative. Finally, you might pose a hypothetical situation that will engage the reader's interest.

Attention-getters can be very brief or extended, depending on the type of business document. Longer documents, those requiring a definite commitment of time by the audience, need more of an attention-getter than shorter, memorandum-type documents.

The second area in the introduction establishes the importance of the written piece to the readers. They need to know why they should read this document. What's special about it? Why should they care about it? In short: What can you (the writer) do for them (the readers)? The more routine, responsive, and informative your writing, the less you need to establish a "need to know" in the reader. In fact, this step is often left out in short, routine, and straightforward memos.

However, the more persuasive your aim, the more you must establish the problem and the need in the reader. Consider, for example, how television affects the daily lives of your readers. As parents and consumers, your readers need to be sensitive to television. Thus, establishing this need in the introduction rivets their attention and gets your writing read.

The third part of a good introduction establishes the thesis of the paper. The thesis, which is generally cast as a declarative sentence, sets forth the writer's perspective on a topic. Presented early in the document, the thesis should set the tone and the focus or direction of the paper for both reader and writer.

Let's look at an example. You might choose the topic of television viewing. One thesis sentence for this subject might be: "Television viewing, while educational in certain circumstances, often incites violent activity in children."

This particular thesis sentence signifies that you will say something specific about the impact of television, and indicates the kind of language you might use in your paper. Right at the start, it gives your readers an idea of the reservations you have about television viewing. In short, the thesis tells the readers something about where your paper is going, and what they can expect.

Usually, you get to the thesis by asking yourself questions that continually seek the focus of your particular topic. This process may require a bullseye approach. Start with a word in an outer ring. Divide the word into its subsequent categories—inner rings. Break these down further and further until you come up with a narrowed focus. This focus will allow both the reader and you, the writer, to target the topic.

The final portion of the introduction contains the pre-summary. This tells the readers specifically what they can expect to read. Using the television example, you might say that first you will cover the questionable educational benefits of television, second the insipid nature of television, and finally the harmful emotional effects that television has on children. Now you have better prepared your readers to follow you on a trip, because now they have a preview of your topic. Further, with the pre-summary, you help create a

mindset within readers, preparing them for
what comes next: the body—the evidence, the
details.

THE BODY

The body represents the second section of
the written document. Imagine that your thesis
sits like a roof on several pillars. The pillars
serve as the buttressed arguments that support
the thesis. Each one of these pillars must relate
directly back to the thesis you're trying to
prove. The pillars themselves should be built
from facts—the bricks and mortar that support
them. In your TV document, the pillars will be
each of the three areas we discussed: the
questionable educational effects of television;
the insipidness of television; and finally the
negative or hostile effects of television.
Because each point derives from your thesis,
the audience has a clear view of your objective
up front. The readers can examine each one of
these main points as you develop them.

Specifically, what supports the main
points? A body of evidence forms the brick and
the mortar for those pillars. You as the builder
organize this information into logically written
paragraphs, themselves constructed like mini

themes (see Chapter 7 for discussion on paragraph construction). Your paragraphs, in turn,
support each pillar or main point and, again, the
main points support your thesis. Thus, you
completely interweave the structure of your
document for strength.

But what about the raw evidence you sup-
ply to build your paragraphs in the body of your
paper? The weight of your supporting information (the evidence) comes in the form of statistics when they are relevant and taken from
reputable sources; quotations when relevant to
the topic and taken from known authorities;
and testimony from those who should know
and those considered to be experts. Personal
experience can movingly illustrate a point, and
personal testimony is effective if the source is
particularly persuasive to readers.

You can organize the body's information
(your evidence) in several ways. First, let's
consider time chronology. Whenever you discuss a process, time sequence provides a good
organizational structure for the body. We might
say that first *A* would happen, then *B* would
occur, and finally *C* would happen. Or in 1964
television did . . ., in 1965 it was . . ., and in
1972 . . .. Or on Monday a certain program

appeared, on Thursday another program appeared, and on Saturday yet a third appeared. Another example uses time vertically within a day (e.g., at 9:00 A.M. a certain show came on; at 10:00 A.M. another one; at 3:00 P.M. another). Time chronologies work well in describing a process, or anything that involves time. Most writers who use the chronological approach usually start with the most distant data and then move toward the present. You can, however, start with the present and move backward.

The second type of structure you might employ is a spatial one, a particularly useful format when you must describe something tangible. Describing a place east or west, north or south, from the front to the back, or from the top to the bottom aids readers when you present a topic.

A third approach, the topical format, is widely used in informative writing and speaking. The television example provides a thesis sentence that contains several topics. It structures the body quite naturally. Using our television example, you would cover the three thesis-related topics you covered in the pre-summary: the questionable educational impact of TV, its insipidness, and its hostile effects.

Remember: Transitions help tie the body together into an understandable whole. Throughout the body, you (as the writer) should tie the main points back to the thesis, thus weaving a tight structure. You can do this by employing specific transitional words that relate directly back to the thesis. For example, you might continue to thread back to your TV thesis by saying, "On the other hand, many people argue that television has its benefits." Words like **moreover, however, also, although**, and others (see Chapter 7) help signal a shift of direction to readers while still maintaining a transitional flow. You can also employ pronouns. For example, you might refer to **television** at the end of one paragraph and then refer to **it** in the next. You can achieve the same effect by using certain words in one paragraph and repeating them in the following one. Each of these transitional techniques serves to unify your writing, giving readers a holistic sense about the piece. Thus, your writing seems coherent and, therefore, more believable.

THE CONCLUSION

Finally, after you have thoroughly developed your main points in the body, you need to sum up your points in a conclusion. First, you should restate your thesis for the readers. Restating the thesis in light of all the detail you've just provided establishes a final and convincing overview for the readers. Next, hammer home the main points that supported your thesis so well. Now your readers can focus all of the evidence presented in the body back onto the thesis. You can do this by reviewing the main points, perhaps by commenting on them while restating the thesis. For example:

> ***Television has brought about many changes in our society, though not all of these societal changes have been good. Television has educated our children in certain rural areas, making it a mainstay of their education. Nonetheless, when examined closely, it is the main, and oftentimes specific, device that fosters illiteracy. Beyond that, recent studies seem to indicate that television may even incite violence in our increasingly violent society.***

With the thesis restated and main points summarized, you offer a final statement that acts as an ending to the writing. Just as you had an opener or attention-getter in your introduction, you ought to have some sort of closing statement. It can come in the form of statistics, quotes, references back to the opening statement, or any other method that will dramatically implant in the reader's mind the implications of what you've just said. In this particular case, perhaps you opened with a dramatic story about a prisoner on death row who said he had seen a murder on television and then copied it. You might want to refer back to him in a dramatic way, perhaps by saying that he still watches television.

STRUCTURE TO STAND ON

All documents need structure in order to stand on their own. That structure includes an introduction, a body, and a conclusion. When writers lace all three together with internal transitions and rhetorical devices, they provide the strength and unity that will hold any document together.

Writing Workshop #8
Rewriting

Now that you've organized your para-graphs, it's time to structure your writing to make it easier for the reader to read. The old standby is appropriate here: Tell them what you want to tell them; tell them; then tell them what you told them. It boils your paper down into three sections: the introduction, the body, and the conclusion.

Objectives

1. To organize a paper that the reader can easily comprehend.

2. To master the principles of a basic rhetori-cal structure.

Activities

STEP 1

Choose an appropriate grabber for your paper. Now provide a statement about why your topic is important to the reader. Next, insert the thesis statement you developed earlier—it will give the reader some direction. Finally, tell the reader what aspects of the thesis you'll cover. Specifically, state the direction the paper will take.

STEP 2

Divide the body of the paper into three or four main points, each of which relate directly to the thesis. Organize the paragraphs and data from previous drafts and exercises to support each of these main points. It's like a pyramid: sentences support main points, and main points support the thesis.

STEP 3

Finally, restate your thesis. Don't repeat it—restate it. Briefly summarize the main points. Finally, end your writing with a good closing. Look to the grabber techniques for ideas. Just make sure you bring the paper to a definite end.

Writing Illustration

NOTE: Since this is a persuasive document, I am going to use a strong "need to know" grabber so the reader gets interested early on.

STEP 1: DEVELOPING THE INTRODUCTION

According to a survey by American Instructors International, after one year of computerized training, most in-house training offices experience a 75 percent increase in the effectiveness of their instructors and efficiency of instruction. Computers are having a strong impact on every facet of American life, and training is no exception.

I believe this percentage of effectiveness and efficiency could be even higher in our Training Office because we have been plagued by a high turnover of instructors. Because of our antiquated office system, our instructors need between six months and a year to become fully effective. Worse, three former instructors who were interviewed for this study said they left the office primarily because they were frustrated by its inefficient systems. Turnover expenses have cost us approximately 25 percent of the budget each year.

Computer expert Mary Jane Byte agrees that the solution to this problem is computerization. In fact, computerization of our training operation would increase both the effectiveness and efficiency of our training unit—two qualities that are looked at strongly by evaluators and auditors every two years.

How can this be done? The plan is simple: Through a computer system that includes different software applications, we can streamline the office system through an indexing and full-text retrieval system, through a database scheduling system, and through computer-based training (CBT) instruction.

STEP 2: WRITING THE BODY OF THE DRAFT

Retrieval System—New instructors must be able to access information and lesson plans on file quickly. Our current word-of-mouth retrieval program—where a new instructor goes to each person in the office for information—is hopelessly obsolete and inefficient. Consequently, new instructors need an inordinate amount of time, oftentimes up to a year, to find out what is available, and even then they are only partially informed. To correct this problem, I suggest a full-text retrieval computer system. Such systems are available for under

$1,000 and will not only produce an indexing system for all items in the file, but will also allow a full-text retrieval through key words. According to Byte, a package called "Quick-Find," which costs approximately $900, will suit our operation perfectly. Quick-Find produces full-text retrieval when words are entered that are contained in the text. Thus, if we entered the term **nonverbal**, we would get all the terms in all the lesson plans that refer to **nonverbal;** however, if we entered **nonverbal** and **hand gestures**, it would sufficiently limit the retrieval to only those references and lesson plans that include both those delineators. This capability would allow new instructors—and old ones—to focus closely on whatever issues are of interest to them.

Scheduling System—As you know, our office works under complicated scheduling loads. Our six instructors are scheduled both on-site and off-site to suit the convenience of our executives. Also, we receive approximately 35 pieces of mail per day that need to be answered, dated, and time-recorded. Currently, we file incoming mail into a particular file with a notation as to the data of the outgoing communication, but we have no way to retrieve this information by name or by date. According to **Computer Match** magazine (June 1995), the software package "Schedule Master" can streamline our office system. This program, which sells for approximately $600, produces an easy-to-use, integrated retrieval system and scheduling system. Byte demonstrated that our secretary could be trained in three days to use this system. We expect its use will improve the efficiency of our office by 40 percent within the first year and by 50 percent within the next year. The savings would be up to $100,000 a year.

Computer-Based Training (CBT)—The teaching of communications breaks down into two general areas: writing communications skills and public speaking communications skills. Both these skills are "doing skills." They require hands-on training as well as drill and practice training.

Hardware—We would need to buy approximately five PCs: one for my office; one at the secretary's desk; two to be shared in the instructors' office area, and one to be used as a server. All terminals would be used for entry and retrieval. A survey conducted by **Computer Match** magazine indicates that the most widely used computer in the training field is the ABC computer system. This computer hardware would cost $20,000.

Software—The three packages necessary are (1) the indexing and full-text retrieval package, Quick-Find ($900); (2) the scheduling/office management system, Schedule Master ($600); (3) and the computer-based training packages ($1,000). The total software costs would be $2,500.

With regard to hands-on training, a variety of exercises, particularly writing exercises, will be enhanced by a computer. According to Stallback (1997), drill-and-practice exercises using a computer in the classroom increase the efficiency of the trainer by at least 25 percent. Thus, by using drill-and-practice packages from ATM Software Inc., the trainer is relieved of purely mechanical responsibilities and can devote his or her time to more vital training. Also, more students can, at the same time, be trained to write well.

With respect to public speaking, two packages are available that review the fundamentals of speech as well as provide diagrams and drill-and-practice. Both packages are put out by the Real-Time Computer Software Company. They cost $500 apiece, but they can save approximately 10 to 15 percent of the teaching time in this course, because they will transmit basic knowledge to executives before they ever enter the classroom. One caveat mentioned by J. Sperling ("Enhancing the Effect of Training," *Communications Hotline* magazine) is that computer training must be integrated with teacher contact. Training exclusively with computers will not be nearly as efficient as integrating it with instructor contact. Therefore, all computer instruction, even at the pre-presentation stage, would be integrated with teacher contact. Students would always be allowed to work solely on their own but not without some supervision and feedback from an instructor.

STEP 3: WRITING THE CONCLUSION

My message is clear: Efficiency and effectiveness can be improved by enhanced computer technology. This effectiveness has been achieved and verified in other companies. I spoke with representatives of four: the Jones and Jones Training Corporation, the Smith and Smith Training Corporation, the XYZ Training Corporation, and the ABC Training Corporation. Each of these companies achieved 30 to 40 percent efficiency improvement as a result of its training, and each sees greater prospects on the horizon. To quote from ***Computer Match*** magazine, "The training operation that does not use computers effectively to assist it is using a 19th-century approach to a 21st-century problem."

9.

TESTING

TESTING

Now that you have joined your research to a solid structure, you should run up a trial balloon of your draft. You need to show your draft to test readers for a reaction. You will find it much easier to clear up ambiguities and miscues **before**, rather than after, you put your work in final form. As the word **testing** implies, this step of the writing process tests your draft on trusted readers who will give you honest feedback.

Think about it. You seek opinions and guidance all the time—when you buy a new dress, a suit, a car, or a boat. It always comforts you to know that you've not been blinded by your own immediate needs and desires.

In this chapter you will learn how to become a writing broker, how to form a writing response group, how to COACH others, and how to use experts to help your writing process.

THE WRITER-BROKER CONCEPT

People often envision a writer as someone who writes in a vacuum. They see a hermit-like figure huddled in a corner with a pen and stack of yellow legal pads—a solitary figure who interacts only with a piece of paper. Wrong! Writers come in all sizes, shapes, and person-alities. And their methods of writing are just as diverse. Sure, writers go through much of the writing process alone. But writing, in fact, is not a solitary process for many, especially when they seek trial reactions from test readers. You need to adopt a writer-broker arrangement.

Writer-brokers function like all other brokers: they coordinate. Brokers bring things together, and most importantly, brokers shoulder the responsibility. Though writer-brokers can delegate any number of functions, in the end they must make the decisions—call the tough shots. So, while writers might ask for the opinions and advice of others, they choose to take or not take that advice. And when advice from others conflicts with your own ideas, decision making can be tough.

Nonetheless, a synergy, a power, comes from involving others in your writing. They can give you a different viewpoint, spot obvious flaws, tell you what works well, and tell you how they, as readers, reacted to your writing.

WRITING RESPONSE GROUPS

To get this reaction to your writing, form your own writing response group. Members can be friends, co-workers, family, or any combination. What's important initially is to have impartial observers read your writing and react to it. Moreover, the closer the group conforms to your selected audience, the more likely you are to get an accurate audience reaction.

How big should you make your response group? Three to five people work well together. Any smaller and you get too little feedback; any larger and you rarely have enough control to get anything done. And how will you expect others to react? How would *you* react in the same circumstances?

THE COACH METHOD

Writing at its best reveals personal ideas. Once you write down your ideas, anyone can look at, inspect, and otherwise critique them— and by implication, *you*. Thus, when you react to another's writing or when others react to your writing, you should know how to respond in a way that will not injure the writer's ego. To help you with this, just remember the word **COACH**: **c**ommend, **o**bserve, **a**sk, **c**onsider, **h**elp.

C—Commend

When you critique another's writing, always offer commendation (praise) first. Why? Because it helps build rapport by relieving the writer's anxiety. Remember, the writer's ego is at risk during the response period. If you make your initial remarks positive, the writer will breathe a sigh of relief, relax, and listen to what you have to say. If, on the other hand, you begin with negative criticism, the writer will feel threatened and experience the fight-or-flight syndrome. First, the writer may fight: bristle and argue, explain, and get defensive. Or the writer will turn to flight: say nothing and wait for the earliest opportunity to bolt, to flee from the discomfort of the session, never to return. In either case, communication between the reader and writer is significantly reduced or severed completely.

When you offer commendations, however, remember to be specific. Avoid generalizing, like, "Your paper was very interesting." Or "You're doing such a great job." Most writers view these kinds of nonspecific praises as hollow, meaningless, and even patronizing. A writer 200 years ago called it "damning with faint praise."

Rather, you should specify exactly what pleases you. For example: "I like the way you clearly explained the function of the committee and how you offered concrete examples about their duties . . .." Or, "Your reasoning about the benefits of the XYZ project showed good, clear, sound logic, especially the part where you . . .." Note how specific praise presents the critic as a sincere and forthright person.

O—Observe

Next, always remain the objective observer. Sometimes you, as the reader, may not like or be interested in the topic. Nonetheless, you must serve as an interested observer for the writer's sake. To help do this, try mentally to role-play the "interested, intelligent ignorant." Imagine yourself as a reader who is generally intelligent, but ignorant about the specific subject. That way you remain open-minded. If you find that too hard, then try to discover something in the writing that you can link with your own life. Look for the positive benefits to yourself. Be an optimist whenever possible.

A—Ask

After building rapport with commendations and objective observations, you can begin to probe the writer with questions. Specifically, when you read a piece of writing and come across a confusing sentence or a place where things don't make sense, put a question mark. Then, at feedback time, pose these questions to the writer. Normally, the question itself will encourage many writers to re-word or clarify the questionable writing. Questions normally don't threaten writers because questions aren't judgmental. Here are some examples of questions you might ask: "What did you mean when you wrote . . .?" "I don't quite understand the relationship between the two main characters. Can you explain it?" "Is there a reason you didn't give the background of the old policy before suggesting a new one?" "Will your targeted audience automatically understand what you mean by . . .?"

Notice how these questions get to the heart of weak points in the writing without necessarily attacking the writer.

C—Consider

Always consider the writer's feelings and intentions. As you already know, writing is an intensely personal endeavor. Writers get involved in their writing and, thus, their feelings come into play. Therefore, always take the softer approach—more considerate, more conservative, less radical—when critiquing someone's work.

H—Help

By this time, if you've used the COACH method, you've earned the right to offer direct help or criticism. Yes, you read correctly. You must **earn the right** to offer help. Sound crazy? Just think about how you use the same approach in your daily life. You'd never think of walking up to a stranger and telling him his tie and suit don't match, but you might tell that to a friend. Friends realize you've got their best interests at heart—even when you criticize.

Thus, after commending, observing, asking, and considering, you have earned the right to offer constructive help. Again, however, offer it in a considerate way: "I think you could make your paper even stronger if you rewrote this part." "I think your introduction was flawless but your conclusion needs a little more work to make it equal in force."

Remember, when offering criticism of any kind, you must first earn the right to do so—a gradual process at best. No blunt critique, no matter how accurate or well intentioned, will be received as well as criticism from those you trust.

EXPERT READERS

To ensure that the substance of your writing is correct, try to test your draft on an expert. For instance, if you're writing about bicycles, a bicycle expert should read your paper for substantive accuracy.

Do you want your bicycle expert to correct your grammar and spelling as well? No, for two reasons. First, your expert may know less than you about writing and the mechanics of English. Second, faced with such a burden, your expert might duck very low to avoid the task. Such editing would intimidate even those experienced at it, let alone a technical expert who may have tried to avoid writing his or her entire life.

So, remove this burden of editing by letting your expert know up front that you want only to "rent" his or her technical brain for a few minutes. You might say, "Donna, I wonder if you would look over this paper and see if I've made any technical errors with respect to bicycles. Don't bother trying to correct the grammar or spelling. I just want your views on the subject matter." Such a preamble will relieve your expert of additional, unwanted responsibilities. It will allow her to do what she does best and to avoid what may well intimidate her.

By becoming a writer-broker and asking both your writing group and a technical expert to review your writing, you can be sure that you're on the right track. Now you're ready for a final proofreading.

Writing Workshop #9
Testing

As a writer, you need feedback before your target audience reads your final product. The testing step will get reactions, raise questions, and further clarify your written piece. By getting reader reactions before you submit the final draft, you give yourself one last chance to revise it for your intended audience.

Objectives

1. To demonstrate the power of groups in the revision process (COACH method).

2. To show the value of expert readers.

Activities

STEP 1

Call together your writing-process group. Give a copy of your draft to each member, then either read your draft aloud or ask them each to read it privately.

Now it's time for reader response, but first be sure to introduce your critics to the COACH rule system:

1. Commend—speak out about what works well.
2. Be Objective—set aside personal biases.
3. Ask—question what you don't understand.
4. Be Considerate—remember the author's feelings.
5. Help—offer suggestions and constructive comments to the author.

STEP 2

Offer your draft to any experts willing to read it. For instance, if the paper is about monetary problems, get an economist and a financial expert to look it over. Make sure they know you're only interested in their comments about your substantive ideas; you aren't looking for their help in grammatical editing.

Writing Illustration

STEP 1: MEETING WITH YOUR WRITING-RESPONSE GROUP

I've developed a small writing response group in my office. Both Jan and Dean are two co-workers I trust. We have agreed to share our drafts. We all adhere to the COACH system and understand that the critiques we give each other are to improve our writing. I gave a copy of my report to each person and asked them to review it and give me their feedback. We sat down for about 15 minutes after they had a chance to look at it. Here's how the meeting went:

First, they both complimented me on the amount of research I had done. Specifically, they liked the way I integrated opinions taken from written sources with oral comments made by the company expert, M.J. Byte. Because she is well respected by management, they thought her endorsement would add credibility to the project. Both added that they thought the project was worthwhile and plausible, and once again praised my foresight and ideas.

Next, they asked me a few questions. First, why didn't I include headers in the text to make it more readable? I told them I forgot, and said I would add them in the next draft. Second, they asked if I had considered having a synopsis up front for the boss. I told them I considered it early on and just forgot it. Third, they asked if I wrote the last draft in two sections. They noted that while the writing in the first half was well done, it seemed to deteriorate somewhat as the memo went on. I admitted that I pushed myself to write the last part late at night and hadn't written it with as much care as I had the first section.

In sum, they suggested that I introduce the memo with a synopsis, add headers, and edit the last part of the draft very closely. I thanked them for their comments and took their edited copies for later referral.

STEP 2: SEEKING SUBSTANTIVE CORROBORATION

I offered the same draft to Mary Jane Byte, our computer expert, to ask for her input. She advised me that the computer hardware, which I had overestimated at $20,000 based on an article from *Computer Match* magazine, would in fact probably cost only $15,000. She showed me various documents that supported this, and I changed my figure to $15,000.

10.

ENDING

ENDING

The time has come for you to finalize your piece of writing. If you've followed the process, you've spent considerable time with your writing, and by now you need to invest only enough time for some final editing and proofing. Some simple strategies can help you clean up your writing, and this chapter lists a number of them for you. As you get more experienced, you'll develop your own editing and proofing strategies. But in the meantime, here are some that will get you started.

ALLOW TIME

Before you do a final reading, let your writing sit for as long as you can. This will help give you a much more objective eye. After you've been away from a piece of writing for a period of time, you'll be surprised at how objectively you can edit your own work.

READ YOUR WRITING ALOUD

To help you self-edit, always read your writing out loud. Wherever you falter during the reading, place a check mark or wavy line and continue reading. Don't stop. Then, once you've finished the reading, go back to the spots you've marked. They will usually be the places where your writing needs revision.

Ideally, you should have someone read your writing aloud to you. You'll be amazed at how differently your writing sounds in another's voice. Problem areas seem to surface quickly and are easy to recognize. If no one is available to read, however, you might record yourself on tape, then play the recording and listen for hesitancies and inconsistencies in the reading. Once again, if you can allow time before replaying the recording, you'll be more objective and may even find that your voice sounds like that of a stranger.

USE THE ACTIVE VOICE

The passive voice seems to have become the norm in business writing. Unfortunately, its use creates bloated and indirect language that is difficult for the reader to understand. For example: "The final plan *was approved* by the committee chairman and *was sent forward* to the executive vice president for his approval." This sentence contains more words than necessary, and its passive construction leaves the reader wondering who sent the program to the vice president. Note what happens if you edit this and put it in the active voice: "Tom Jones, the committee chairman, **_approved_** the final plan and **_sent_** it to the executive vice president for his approval." Now the sentence is clear and so is the responsibility.

Review your writing and look for either implied or direct use of the passive voice. To help you spot the passive voice, note all the by's in your writing. They usually indicate that a passive construction is lurking nearby. Then, recast the sentence in the active voice, and see how it makes a stronger, more direct sentence that the reader can more easily comprehend.

AVOID THE VERB "IS"

Like the passive voice, the verb **_is_** or **_to be_**, in all of its forms, creates weak writing. **_Is_**, like the other so-called linking verbs (**_appear, become, seem, feel, grow, act, look, taste, smell, sound_**), merely links subjects with adjectives or objects and avoids any action. On the other hand, strong, active verbs add life to any sentence. Too many linking verbs will cut out the life and dilute the power of your writing.

Dull: The dog appeared happy when he saw the young boy. The boy was young and cute and acted like a typical boy as he got off the bus.

Alive: The dog vigorously wagged his tail, eagerly awaiting the boy. The eight-year-old, blond-haired boy jumped off the bus, chasing a friend while yelling at the top of his lungs.

The second sentence allows you to picture in your mind a loving dog waiting for his lively young master. The first sentence leaves you flat; you can't "see" any picture. By using active verbs, you help the reader see the action: *Wagged, jumped, yelling* all help the writing come alive. Admittedly, the adjectives placed next to the nouns also help, but the verbs create the action, something your mind's eye picks up naturally.

USE SHORT SENTENCES — THE RULE OF TWENTY

Look at any piece of writing, and if you see more than three lines of typing without a period or semi-colon, chances are you'll start getting confused. More than twenty words in a sentence leads to reader confusion. So reread what you've written, note with a wavy line in the margin where you see lengthy sentences, and go back to revise them. There are several ways to trim excess writing fat: cut prepositional phrases, look for restatements that add nothing to your writing, and, *avoid the passive voice.*

Cut prepositional phrases such as: *along the lines of, as of this date, at the present time,* and *in the event that*; instead, use *like*, *today*, *now*, and *if*. Locate a prepositional phrase, and ask yourself if you can use one word where you've written three. Whenever you see the preposition *of*, see if you can use the possessive to eliminate a couple of words:

Bloated: The meeting was held in the office of the president.

Trimmed: The meeting was held in the president's office.

You also can trim language by looking for obvious restatements or for words that have a double meaning:

Redundant: The staffers got together and did some advance planning; that is, they put their heads together to find solutions.

Efficient: The staffers met and planned strategies.

Finally, look again for the passive voice. A prepositional phrase usually introduces it, and by eliminating the phrase you can trim back the sentence:

Passive: The market is dictated by the large investors.

Active: Large investors affect the market.

The first sentence contains eight words, the second only five—that's a large savings in words.

DON'T SMOTHER VERBS

Don't camouflage verbs, or you'll lose the action and flavor of your sentences. To clean up hidden verbs, try this tip: underline words ending with *-ent, -ant, -ion, -ment, -ence, -ance,* or *-ency*. Writers frequently place these endings on verbs to make them nouns, thereby destroying their action.

Hidden: The instructor made the standing assignment for implementation of better productivity of students.

Clear: The instructor assigned regular homework to ensure student productivity.

Notice that when you eliminate muffled words like ***assignment*** and ***implementation***, the sentence shortens and comes alive.

USE CONCRETE LANGUAGE

Abstract language continues to creep into corporate writing. Vague, imprecise language paints a fuzzy picture. You can paint a crystal-clear picture by asking yourself the old standby questions: Who? What? When? Where? Why? How?

Fuzzy: The supervisor of one of our units possesses the proper skills to navigate an aerospace vehicle.

Clear: Our contracts manager can fly planes.

Notice how the second sentence gets right to the meat of the issue, letting you know who can do what. Also, remember the KIS principle: Keep it simple.

KEEP RELATED WORDS TOGETHER

Misplaced modifiers cause readers heartburn. They have to reread to figure out what you're trying to say, or worse, they misunderstand.

> *Misplaced:* After months of traveling, the secretary met with her boss at the airport.

> *Clearer:* After months of traveling, the boss met his secretary at the airport.

Notice that in the first sentence you may have thought the secretary was doing all the traveling. Not so. It was the boss's homecoming.

To eliminate this common problem, always place the modifier (adverb, adjective, or prepositional phrase) nearest the word it modifies.

Foggy: The boss discussed the problem in the men's room.

Clearer: In the men's room the boss discussed the problem.

By moving the prepositional phrase, you change the meaning of the sentence. After all, the problem was not in the men's room—it was only discussed there.

Avoid Shifts

Avoid shifts in number, tense, sex, subject, or point of view.

Number

Subjects should always match their verbs and pronouns. Plural subjects take plural verbs and pronouns.

Mixed numbers: The engineer asked if they could come in the room to perform their tests.

In line: The engineer asked if he could come into the room to perform his tests.

Tense

Shifting verb tenses also confuses readers:

Time problem: The supervisor viewed the dispute and breaks it up.

On time: The supervisor saw the fight and broke it up.

Sex

Beware of sex-biased words in your writing. Certain titles or words deny women the stature they deserve. Avoid male-dominated titles like policeman and workman in favor of more generic terms: police officer or worker. To avoid sex-biased language, use plural subjects:

Not: Each worker took off his hard hat.

But: The workers took off their hard hats.

Whatever strategy you use in your writing, avoid sexist language whenever possible.

Subject

Changing the subject in midsentence throws the reader off course. Avoid any shift in subject when possible:

Not: The copy editor finished the document, and it was rewritten.

But: The copy editor finished the documents; then she had it rewritten.

DETERMINE THE POINT OF VIEW

The point of view gives the reader a perspective of who is telling the story. Some people write memos and reports from an "I" or first-person perspective; others write them from a "you" or second-person perspective (like this book); and still others write from a "he, she, or they" or third-person perspective. Each perspective is the point of view, and shifting it in your writing confuses readers:

Not: The manager said that when I read the memo, you could see the mistakes that we had made.

But: The manager said that when he read the memo, he could see the mistakes.

MAKE YOUR WRITING READABLE

White space is that blank area on a printed page. White space provides eye relief to the reader. Pick up most single-spaced legal documents, for example, and you'll usually find very little white space—little eye relief. As a result, readers tend to avoid such documents. When was the last time you took out your life insurance policy or the deed to the house and read it for pleasure?

By creating white space in a piece of writing, you make it more readable and, thus, it will be read more often. Also, if well formatted with white space, your document will look more organized, leaving a much better impression on the reader. That is very important in business.

To create white space and to order your writing, try these tips:

- Indent the main points.
- Underline to stress a point.
- Use bullets and lists.

- Always double-space, but if you must single-space, skip two lines between paragraphs.
- Design short paragraphs
- Break up text with illustrations.
- Break up space and provide shifts in the text with liberal use of subheadings.
- Number items in lists or number major points you want to make.

LETTING GO

Finally, after you have finished all your work, after you and your group or friend have proofed and re-proofed your writing, it's time to submit it and wait for the results. Once you have finished your piece of writing, don't be surprised if you feel a little down. When you invest so much of yourself in anything, you will have a hard time letting it go. Many business people feel somewhat depressed when they complete a particularly long document. It's been such a big part of them for so long. What's the cure? Start writing something new. Good luck!

Writing Workshop #10
Ending

Now it's time to check your paper for mechanics. You've held off doing this until now to save time. Check for spelling, punctuation, grammar, and format. When you're done, submit it and end the process.

Objective

To prepare a final document for submission.

Activities

STEP 1

First, re-read Chapter 10 in this book. Note all the tips. Now go through your draft, using these tips to make sure you have: used direct, useful verbs; kept sentences short; avoided abstractions; kept related words together; not shifted number, tense, sex, subject, or point of view; and used solid construction in your writing.

Read your draft out loud and into a tape recorder, if you have one. Wherever you stumble, mark the spot, but don't stop reading. When you're done, go back to the spots you checked. Chances are good that those pencil-marked places will point to problems in your writing.

STEP 2
A job well done—Congratulations!

Writing Illustration

STEP 1: MEMORANDUM REPORT—FINAL

TO: Joan Jones, Director of Training

FROM: Raymond Stark, Chief of
Communication Instruction Office

DATE: 2/2/99

SUBJECT: COMPUTER ENHANCEMENTS TO
COMMUNICATION INSTRUCTION
TO IMPROVE EFFICIENCY AND
EFFECTIVENESS

Report Synopsis

We currently have an inefficient training system in our Communication Instruction Office. Turnover of instructors, a lack of full-text retrieval systems, and no effective computer-based training (CBT) methods—all are causing a noticeable decrease in the efficiency and effectiveness of the office. Documented research shows that computerization could increase our efficiency by 25 percent. Computers can improve our operation in several areas: lesson plan indexing and retrieval, scheduling, and CBT instruction.

Details

According to a survey by American Instructors International, after one year of computerized training, most in-house training offices experience a 25 percent increase in the effectiveness of their instructors and in the efficiency of their instruction.

I believe the increase in efficiency could be even greater in our Training Office because we have been plagued by a high turnover of instructors. Because of our antiquated office system, our instructors need between six months and a year to become effective. Worse, three former instructors who were interviewed for this study said they left the office primarily because they were frustrated by its inefficient systems. Turnover expenses have cost us approximately 25 percent of the budget each year. Computer expert Mary Jane Byte agrees that the solution to this problem is computerization. In fact, computerization of our training operation would increase both the effectiveness and efficiency of our training unit—two qualities that are looked at strongly by evaluators and auditors every two years.

How can this be done? The plan is simple: We can streamline the office system with a computer system that includes different software applications: an indexing and full-text retrieval system, a scheduling system, and computer-based training (CBT).

Indexing and Full-Text Retrieval

New instructors must be able to access information and lesson plans quickly. Our current word-of-mouth retrieval program— where a new instructor goes to each person in the office for information—is hopelessly obsolete and inefficient. Consequently, new instructors need an inordinate amount of time to find out what is available. Even then they are only partially informed.

To correct this problem I suggest a full-text retrieval system. Such systems are available for under $1,000. In addition to producing an indexing system for all items in the file, they also allow a full-text retrieval through key-words. According to Ms. Byte, a software package called "Quick-Find," which costs approximately $900, will suit our operation perfectly. Quick-Find produces full-text retrieval when words are entered that are contained in the text. Thus, if we entered the term **nonverbal**, we would get all the references in all the lesson plans that use **nonverbal**; however, if we entered **nonverbal** and **hand gestures**, it would sufficiently limit the retrieval to only those references and lesson plans that include both those delineators. This capability would allow new instructors—and old ones—to focus closely on whatever issues are of interest to them.

Office Management Scheduling System

As you know, our office works under complicated scheduling loads. Our six instructors are scheduled to teach both on-site and off-site to suit the convenience of our executives. Also, we receive approximately 35 pieces of mail per day that need to be answered, dated, and tracked. Currently, we have no way to retrieve mail information by name or by date. According to **Computer Match** magazine, June 1995, the software package "Schedule Master" can streamline our office system. This program, which sells for approximately $600, produces an easy-to-use, integrated retrieval and scheduling system. Ms. Byte demonstrated that our secretary could be trained in three days to use this system. We expect its use will improve the efficiency of our office by 10 percent within the first year and by 20 percent within the next year. The savings will add up to $100,000 in the years to come. Further, the quality of communication instruction would significantly improve.

Computer-Based Training (CBT)

Our teaching of communications breaks down into two major general areas: writing communication skills and public-speaking communication skills. Both of these skills are "doing skills." They require hands-on training as well as drill-and-practice training. For the hands-on training, a variety of exercises, particularly writing exercises, will be enhanced by a CBT. For example, according to Stallbach (1997), computer-based training exercises in the classroom increase the efficiency of the trainer by at least 10 percent. Thus, by using a CBT package such as the one provided by ATM Software Inc., of New Jersey, more students can receive more training, with less drain on instructors. The instructors, therefore, will have more time to give individual help to those who need it.

Two CBT packages are available that review the fundamentals of speech and provide drill and practice for oral communications. These packages are marketed by the Real-Time Computer Software Company and cost $500 apiece. I estimate that they will save approximately 10 to 15 percent of the teaching time in our public-speaking course, and will give executives foundation knowledge of the subject before ever coming to class. One caveat mentioned in J. Sperling's article "Enhancing the Effect of Training" in *Communications Hotline* magazine, May 1998, is that CBT must be integrated with teacher contact. Exclusive CBT will not be nearly as effective as computer training coupled with instructor training. Therefore, we would never use these packages as replacements for our teacher-based training.

Purchasing Needs

To meet our computer needs, we will need to buy approximately five PCs (one server and four work stations). One work station will be put in my office; one will be placed at the secretary's desk; and the two others will be put in the instructors' office area. All work stations will, if purchased, be used for entry and retrieval. A recent survey conducted by *Computer Match* magazine indicates that the most widely used computer in the training field is the ABC computer system. This computer hardware would cost $15,000.

Software—The three packages necessary are (1) the indexing and full-text retrieval package, Quick-Find ($900); (2) the scheduling/

office management system, Schedule Master
($600); and (3) the two computer-based train-
ing packages ($1,000). The total software
costs would be $2,500.

Recommendation

Computer equipment will clearly improve
the efficiency and effectiveness of our office
operations. In fact, I have found four other
training companies that have tested the value
of a similar system: the Jones and Jones
Training Corporation, the Smith and Smith
Training Corporation, the XYZ Training
Corporation, and the ABC Training Corporation.
All of these companies achieved a 30 to 40
percent efficiency improvement as a result of
their training and see even greater prospects on
the horizon. To quote from **Computer Match**
magazine, "The training operation that does not
use computers effectively is no longer viable—
it is using a 19th-century approach to solve a
21st-century problem."

**Therefore, I recommend purchasing the
equipment outlined in the "Purchasing Needs"
section of this memo as soon as the budget
process allows.**

ABOUT THE AUTHOR

Steve Gladis, Ph.D.

The varied career of Dr. Steve Gladis includes academic, government, and military experience as well as civic service.

Dr. Gladis is a member of the University of Virginia's faculty and serves as the director of the University's Northern Virginia Center, which serves over 7,000 students with over 500 courses and programs. In his previous career, Dr. Gladis served as a Special Agent in the FBI. He taught at the FBI Academy, was the editor of the *FBI Law Enforcement Bulletin*, served as the chief of speechwriting for the director of the FBI, and held a number of both headquarters and field-agent assignments around the country. He is also a former U.S. Marine Corps officer and a Vietnam Veteran.

Dr. Gladis has published numerous magazine and journal articles as well as eight books. A regular lecturer and speaker, Dr. Gladis consults with corporations and organizations in the area of training and development.

A committed civic and academic leader, Dr. Gladis serves on the Executive Board of the Fairfax County Chamber of Commerce, is the chairman of the Board of Trustees of the Washington Math Science Technology Public Charter High School, and is a member of the University of Virginia's Faculty Senate.